Ne

MW00761766

BEATS IN TIME
A Literary Generation's Legacy

A Literary Kicks Collection
Edited by Levi Asher

Beat Generation – Literary History – Essays

Published by Literary Kicks
328 8th Avenue #337
New York NY 10001 USA

Cover illustration by David Richardson

First Edition (v2.2) July 2011

Ah, Carl, while you are not safe I am not safe, and now you're really in the total animal soup of time ...
– Allen Ginsberg, "Howl"

Table of Contents

INTRODUCTION
by Levi Asher

It took the world forty years to catch on to the writers of the Beat Generation.

Born roughly October 1955 with Allen Ginsberg's performance of "Howl" at the Six Gallery in San Francisco, the ambitious literary revolution plotted by Ginsberg, Jack Kerouac, John Clellon Holmes and Lawrence Ferlinghetti destroyed itself in a few short years, floundering into irrelevance by the end of the 1950s amidst media ridicule and terrible reviews. By 1959, when a goofy "beatnik" character named Maynard G. Krebs appeared on a TV sitcom called "The Many Loves of Dobie Gillis", the Beat Generation label had become a liability for any writer who wanted his work taken seriously.

The Beats themselves – a small group of earnest, brilliant writers who had originally coalesced around Columbia University in the 1940s – suffered terribly for their quick leap to fame and descent into cliché. Jack Kerouac's writing career never had a second act, nor Gregory Corso's. Several Beat authors eventually managed to build strong literary reputations, but only did so by shedding the label and finding new gigs: Allen Ginsberg became a hippie and a peace activist, William S. Burroughs a stylish experimental postmodernist, Lawrence Ferlinghetti an innovative publisher of international fiction, Gary Snyder an academy poet and writing professor.

A LITERARY GENERATION'S LEGACY

For decades, "Beat" was a forgotten thing -- gone, nowhere. The renaissance was slow in coming. I was lucky to watch it happen, and maybe even help it along.

When I launched a webpage called Literary Kicks, featuring a few short biographies of the major Beat writers, in the summer of 1994, I had no reason to think I would find an audience. The Beat Generation had still gained little traction among academics or critics at this time. Jack Kerouac was dead a quarter century, many of his books out of print. Allen Ginsberg was still around, still publishing those City Lights books that everybody loved and nobody bought, tirelessly nursing his reputation with downtown poetry readings and occasional angry New York Times editorials. He was an inspiring presence within the New York Poetry scene, but hardly the "most famous poet" in America that he would seem to always have been when he suddenly died three years later. In the summer of 1994, you'd be lucky to find a single "Beat Generation" book in a bookstore, and if you found one it would almost certainly be written by Ann Charters.

In retrospect, it feels like I must have been pulled along by some mysterious *zeitgeist* on the day I created this website, because the Beat Generation was poised to suddenly explode in popular interest and academic appreciation. This possibility was not remotely on my mind when I created Literary Kicks. As a software developer with an interest in fiction and poetry, I built the website as an experiment in the new field of web publishing. I chose to write about the Beat Generation only because I happened to be reading a biography of Jack Kerouac at the time. I figured I'd finish this website and build a new one about

Franz Kafka, or James Joyce, or Herman Melville a week or two later. I never got the chance.

Instead, Literary Kicks seemed to resonate with readers the minute it was launched. My web counter hit 100 pageviews on the very first day, and reached quadruple digits within a few months. Yahoo!, then the most popular web search engine, put me at the top of a "Beat Generation" directory page, funneling new readers my way. Why were they all searching for "Beat Generation"? I had no idea, but they were.

Then newspapers and magazines started mentioning my site in Internet culture round-ups, though I often wished they would stop talking about bongos. "Grab your bongos and check out Literary Kicks" said *MacUser* in an April 1995 article about book websites. A year later the site was listed in *Wired*: "Bust out your bongos and light up a cig – it's time to dig the Beat Generation." Similar notices began appearing in the *New York Times*, the *Village Voice*, *Los Angeles Times*, *Chicago Tribune*, *San Francisco Chronicle*, *Time Out London*. Amazingly, the journalists who wrote these articles seemed to regard a Beat literature website as something fresh, something relevant to today.

As the webmaster and sole editorial voice behind this suddenly popular site, I had to scramble to catch up with my own topic. I was far from knowledgeable about the Beat Generation when I launched the site. I furiously read up on Gregory Corso, Gary Snyder, Philip Whalen, Ted Joans, Bob Kaufman and Michael McClure so that nobody would find out I was a fake.

3

A LITERARY GENERATION'S LEGACY

Contributions from worthy authors like John Perry Barlow and Don Carpenter began to flow my way, and I expanded the site to include book reviews, poems, a news section, a few jokes. Eventually my knowledge about the Beat writers began to catch up with my reputation.

Why did popular interest in the Beat writers suddenly increase in the mid-1990s? There seemed to be some resonance with the age of Starbucks and grunge. The old novels and poetry chapbooks were connecting with young readers in ways that must have echoed the original Beatnik craze of the late 1950s.

As the level of interest grew, publishers began to put out new biographies, literary studies and reissues of out-of-print Beat Generation books. New York University put on a Beat Generation conference, and the Whitney Museum launched a travelling exhibit on Beat Art. Francis Ford Coppola announced plans to film Jack Kerouac's *On The Road*, and Kerouac began showing up in Gap ads. Allen Ginsberg died in 1997, to far greater media fanfare than anyone would have expected only a few years earlier, and his close friend William S. Burroughs died a few months later, also eliciting a broad public reaction. You could now find five books about the Beat Generation in a bookstore … then ten, and then a whole shelf.

By the beginning of the 2000s, Jack Kerouac was a household name, and many college English departments were offering courses in Beat 101. Shoppers could find Beat CD-Roms, beatnik t-shirts, Beat fonts. I remember the day Literary Kicks got a mention in *Vogue* magazine, and I thought "this has gone too far."

How does a literary movement invent itself over time? We can often learn as much by studying popular perceptions of body of literary work as we can by studying the work itself, and the emergence of a sudden new interest in the Beat writers between the mid-1990s and the early 2000s presents a great petri dish for such a study. The articles, interviews, essays and tributes in this book all appeared originally on Literary Kicks during the years that many readers around the world were discovering the Beat writers for the first time, and they can be read today, not only for their intrinsic interest, but as snapshots of a shared public awareness that was quickly growing and changing.

These articles, and the website as a whole, may have helped to give the old tired "Beat" image a new kick. The site was clearly styled as a product of its own time, not a throwback to the past. We sought fresh connections above all, taking every opportunity to compare Beat writers to their contemporary equivalents, and maintaining a growing list of dozens, then hundreds of Beat references in current music (10,000 Maniacs sang about Kerouac, Kurt Cobain recorded with Burroughs, Cornershop jammed with Ginsberg, Red Hot Chili Peppers shouted out to Bukowski on "Blood Sex Sugar Magic") or on television shows (as when Jack Kerouac suddenly turned up in an episode of the sci-fi action-drama "Quantum Leap").

Most importantly, our articles took the Beat writers seriously, even when we criticized their work. There are wildly varying

5

voices and points of view in the pieces selected for this book, but the common theme among all is the emergence of a timeless view of Beat literature. Like a few lucky generations before (the British Romantics, the New England Transcendentalists, the French Symbolists, the Pre-Raphaelites, the Jazz-Age Modernists), between 1994 and 2005 the Beat Generation emerged as something serious, meaningful, distinct.

This is an occasion that happens only rarely in literary history. It's painful to watch generations strain to become legendary (like the "Brat Pack" of the 1980s – Jay McInerney, Bret Easton Ellis, Tama Janowitz – which tried so hard). We witnessed some kind of remarkable breakthrough in the years after 1994 (the years covered in this book), and I hope "Beats In Time" can help to illuminate what this breakthrough actually was.

Did the Beat Generation also lose something by becoming a cliche, by growing old, by suddenly earning lots of money? Probably. The question of the commercialization and Hollywood-ization of Beat literature is a thorny topic, and several of the pieces in this book grapple with the moral side effects of this sudden new popularity, as well as the moral side effects of the wealth it generated, for the benefit of some more than others.

The articles in this book are arranged in the order that they were originally published. It begins with Grateful Dead lyricist John Perry Barlow's memoir of Neal Cassady, and of the song "Cassidy". Barlow originally wrote this article for an online discussion group, but the memorable piece has found a permanent home on its Litkicks page, and is significant to anyone interested in the longstanding relationship between the Beat Generation and the Grateful Dead.   Early in their career, the Dead befriended Neal Cassady and late-Beat novelist Ken Kesey, and the band kept the candle burning with lyrical references to Beat themes in several songs. These musical connections helped stoke my own early interest in the Beat writers, so it meant a lot to me to run this piece.

The second piece in this book tells the story of what happened in early 1995 when I auditioned for Francis Ford Coppola's new movie version on Kerouac's *On The Road.* Incredibly, as of this writing, in the summer of 2011, this same movie version of *On The Road* is finally scheduled to be released, and will appear in theaters hopefully by the end of this year. I have no idea what took the filmmakers so long. I didn't get the part.

Next, "Ringside Seat" describes a shocking scene I witnessed around the first major academic conference devoted to the Beat Generation in New York City. The sudden new popularity of Jack Kerouac had led to a financial windfall, unfortunately also leading to an ugly, explosive battle that pitted Kerouac's ailing daughter against his literary estate.

For many starry-eyed Kerouac readers like me, the spectacle of the novelist's heirs squabbling over money in public stood as a depressing repudiation of Kerouac's own message of grace, spiritual generosity and Buddhist poverty. The feud revolving around the Kerouac estate would go on for years, and I had to struggle to keep Literary Kicks from getting drawn in to the ever-growing drama. I often did this by turning my attention back to the literary past. One of my favorite early pieces in this vein is "John Montgomery, Dharma Bum", a portrait by Jim Stedman of an elderly hipster/outdoorsman who had once been enshrined as the comic character Henry Morley in Jack Kerouac's novel *Dharma Bums*.

In its first few years my website served as a magnet for Beat survivors – at least those who could figure out how to use email – and I was thrilled to make contact with Neal Cassady's son John, who was eager to speak for the first time in public about his experiences as a child of the Beat Generation. I also heard from the daughter of writer Don Carpenter, who gave me a delightful chapter from her father's unpublished memoir.

My favorite piece in this book may be the long record of the spontaneous reaction to the announcement of Allen Ginsberg's fatal illness and death that took place on the BEAT-L mailing list in April 1997. While this group exchange is long and ragged (what good online discussion is not?), its lengthy excessiveness feels appropriate for its unabashedly self-indulgent subject. Some of the expressions of poetic *exstatis* during this long exchange strain credulity today, but it was always Ginsberg's genius to never be embarrassed to express everything, to risk pretentiousness and let his thoughts flow into their natural state of beauty. Many shocked and saddened Allen Ginsberg aficionados let their thoughts flow during this recorded conversation – an even longer version of which has been widely shared and enjoyed online as a memorial to his death.

This rambling exchange also shows the powerful spark of a wider convergence that was taking place during these years: the coming together of literary culture and Internet culture, producing a new "Interzone" that happily adopted the Beat writers among its heroes. The fact that Internet culture loves the Beats is great for the Beat legacy. Perhaps more importantly, the fact that Internet culture loves the Beats is great for Internet culture.

This tribute is followed by another tribute, in a different format, to William S. Burroughs, including a haunting account of his Kansas death ceremony by his friend Patricia Elliot. A number of other Beat writers, including Ray Bremser, Herbert Huncke and Ken Kesey would die in the following several years, making the late 1990s and early 2000s feel like a long season of memorial tributes for fans of the Beat Generation. But the sad farewells enriched Literary Kicks, as we continued to collect spontaneous and heartfelt tributes to bygone writers from those that knew them or their works intimately. Three more tributes are included in this book. First, Ray Freed recalls his friend Jack Micheline, the street poet from San Francisco, who died on a BART train in 1998.

Since I'd begun absorbing myself in Beat literature a few years earlier, the great poet Gregory Corso had become a personal favorite of mine. He died in January 2001, and rather than gather a tribute page from contributions emailed to me I tried something new on my website: a message board devoted to Corso's memory, where anybody with something to share could post their words directly on my site. A few of the most

9

memorable posts from this tribute board have been selected for the "Corso Collage" in this book. These include several short memory fragments sent in by Graham Seidman, who had been Corso's friend and housemate in Paris and Puerto Rico. Several poems in the Corso tribute also show a trend I observed during the Allen Ginsberg tribute vigil in 1997: while the BEAT-L vigil seemed to follow in Ginsberg's long-breathed, majestic style, the poems written for Gregory Corso often recalled Corso's own puckish, freewheeling poetic voice. If there's any doubt about the deep positive influence Allen Ginsberg and Gregory Corso had on new generations of younger readers, the evidence of these tribute poems speaks for itself.

The last tribute in this series of memorials is Laki Vazakas's biographical sketch of poet Marty Matz, a poet I enjoyed meeting and hearing at various New York City poetry events before he died.

I began to steer Literary Kicks away from its exclusive focus on Beat writing in the early 2000s, sensing that I was no longer providing anything distinctly original. I still accepted worthy Beat-related articles from contributors like Joseph Matheny, who had interviewed Diane DiPrima about magick, poetry and politics years before, and Jamelah Earle, who wrote about the environmental messages in Gary Snyder's poetry and then conducted an email interview with Black Mountain poet Robert Creeley shortly before his death in 2005. Creeley had taken a special interest in the artistic potential of digital and Internet-connected literature, and this interview highlights his innovative ideas about this topic.

October 7, 2005 was the 50th anniversary of the seminal Six Gallery poetry reading in San Francisco that had started it all. California poet Michael McClure (who, of course, was there) was kind enough to respond to my request for his thoughts on this anniversary: "What It Meant".

After noticing the increasing popularity of poet W. S. Merwin, who won a National Book Award in 2005, I wrote "When Hippies Battle" in order to explore a strange legend I'd heard about a confrontation between the nature poet and a famous Buddhist teacher that had taken place thirty years earlier at Allen Ginsberg and Anne Waldman's Naropa Institute. I'm not sure if there's any moral to the sordid tale I eventually pieced together from various biographical sources -- and maybe that's what draws me to the story..

Jazz musician and Beat happener David Amram has always been a good friend to Literary Kicks, and Bill Ectric's interview with Amram captures the warmth and sparkle that everybody who's had the privilege of meeting or jamming with David already knows well.

Beats In Time ends with your humble editor in a Brooklyn coffeehouse interviewing the charming Venice Beach/Los Angeles scene poet and former nun Philomene Long. Philomene died the following summer.

I feel great affection for every one of the eighteen pieces in this book, but it's the small portraits, like Jim Stedman's sketch of

A LITERARY GENERATION'S LEGACY

wood-choppin' Jim Montgomery, or Don Carpenter's piquant memory of a chaotic poetry event, or my interview with Philomene Long in the year before her death, that hold the most significance for me, and seem to best represent what the Beat spirit has stood for since its earliest days.

I don't know if many of the rambling hipsters or intrepid latter-day beatniks represented here will ever make it into many literary anthologies. But I hope they do, and I hope it means something that they made it into this book. These are the writers who kept it real – even during the long decades when nobody cared.

CASSIDY'S TALE

by John Perry Barlow

I have seen where the wolf has slept by the silver stream.
I can tell by the mark he left you were in his dream.
Ah, child of countless trees.

Ah, child of boundless seas.
What you are, what you're meant to be
Speaks his name, though you were born to me,

Born to me,
Cassidy...

Lost now on the country miles in his Cadillac.
I can tell by the way you smile he's rolling back.
Come wash the nighttime clean,
Come grow this scorched ground green,
Blow the horn, tap the tambourine
Close the gap of the dark years in between
You and me,

Cassidy...

Quick beats in an icy heart.
Catch-colt draws a coffin cart.
There he goes now, here she starts:

Hear her cry.
Flight of the seabirds, scattered like lost words
Wheel to the storm and fly.

Faring thee well now.
Let your life proceed by its own design.
Nothing to tell now.

A LITERARY GENERATION'S LEGACY

Let the words be yours, I'm done with mine.
– "Cassidy" by Bob Weir and John Perry Barlow

This is a song about necessary dualities: dying and being born, men and women, speaking and being silent, devastation and growth, desolation and hope.

It is also about a Cassady and a Cassidy, Neal Cassady and Cassidy Law.

(The title could be spelled either way as far as I'm concerned, but I think it's officially stamped with the latter. Which is appropriate since I believe the copyright was registered by the latter's mother, Eileen Law.)

The first of these was the ineffable, inimitable, indefatigable Holy Goof Hisself, Neal Cassady, aka Dean Moriarty, Hart Kennedy, Houlihan, and The Best Mind of Allen Ginsberg's generation.

Neal Cassady, for those whose education has been so classical or so trivial or so timid as to omit him, was the Avatar of American Hipness. Born on the road and springing full-blown from a fleabag on Denver's Larimer Street, he met the hitch-hiking Jack Kerouac there in the late 40's and set him, and, through him, millions of others, permanently free.

Neal came from the oral tradition. The writing he left to others with more time and attention span, but from his vast reserves flowed the high-octane juice which gassed up the Beat Generation for eight years of Eisenhower and a thousand days

14

of Camelot until it, like so many other things, ground to a bewildered halt in Dallas.

Kerouac retreated to Long Island, where he took up Budweiser, the *National Review*, and the adipose cynicism of too many thwarted revolutionaries. Neal just caught the next bus out.

This turned out to be the psychedelic nose-cone of the 60's, a rolling cornucopia of technicolor weirdness named Further. With Ken Kesey raving from the roof and Neal at the wheel, Further roamed America from 1964 to 1966, infecting our national control delusion with a chronic and holy lunacy to which it may yet succumb.

From Further tumbled the Acid Tests, the Grateful Dead, Human Be-Ins, the Haight-Ashbury, and, as America tried to suppress the infection by popularizing it into cheap folly, The Summer of "Love" and Woodstock.

I, meanwhile, had been initiated into the Mysteries within the sober ashrams of Timothy Leary's East Coast, from which distance the Prankster's psychedelic psircuses seemed, well, a bit psacreligious. Bobby Weir, whom I'd known since prep school, kept me somewhat current on his riotous doings with the Pranksters et al, but I tended to dismiss on ideological grounds what little of this madness he could squeeze through a telephone.

So, purist that I was, I didn't actually meet Neal Cassady until 1967, by which time Further was already rusticating behind

15

A LITERARY GENERATION'S LEGACY

Kesey's barn in Oregon and the Grateful Dead had collectively beached itself in a magnificently broke-down Victorian palace at 710 Ashbury Street, two blocks up the hill from what was by then, according to Time Magazine, the axis mundi of American popular culture. The real party was pretty much over by the time I arrived.

But Cassady, the Most Amazing Man I Ever Met, was still very much Happening. Holding court in 710's tiny kitchen, he would carry on five different conversations at once and still devote one conversational channel to discourse with absent persons and another to such sound effects as disintegrating ring gears or exploding crania. To log into one of these conversations, despite their multiplicity, was like trying to take a sip from a fire hose.

He filled his few and momentary lapses in flow with the most random numbers ever generated by man or computer or, more often, with his low signature laugh, a "heh, heh, heh, heh" which sounded like an engine being spun furiously by an over-enthusiastic starter motor.

As far as I could tell he never slept. He tossed back green hearts of Mexican dexedrina by the shot-sized bottle, grinned, cackled, and jammed on into the night. Despite such behavior, he seemed, at 41, a paragon of robust health. With a face out of a recruiting poster (leaving aside a certain glint in the eyes) and a torso, usually raw, by Michelangelo, he didn't even seem quite mortal. Though he would shortly demonstrate himself to be so.

Neal and Bobby were perfectly contrapuntal. As Cassady rattled incessantly, Bobby had fallen mostly mute, stilled perhaps by macrobiotics, perhaps a less than passing grade in the Acid Tests, or, more likely, some combination of every strange thing which had caused him to start thinking much faster than anyone could talk. I don't have many focussed memories from the Summer of 1967, but in every mental image I retain of Neal, Bobby's pale, expressionless face hovers as well.

Their proximity owed partly to Weir's diet. Each meal required hours of methodical effort. First, a variety of semi-edibles had to be reduced over low heat to a brown, gelatinous consistency. Then each bite of this preparation had to be chewed no less than 40 times. I believe there was some ceremonial reason for this, though maybe he just needed time to get used to the taste before swallowing.

This all took place in the kitchen where, as I say, Cassady was also usually taking place. So there would be Neal, a fountain of language, issuing forth clouds of agitated, migratory words. And across the table, Bobby, his jaw working no less vigorously, producing instead a profound, unalterable silence. Neal talked. Bobby chewed. And listened.

So would pass the day. I remember a couple of nights when they set up another joint routine in the music room upstairs. The front room of the second floor had once been a library and was now the location of a stereo and a huge collection of communally-abused records.

A LITERARY GENERATION'S LEGACY

It was also, at this time, Bobby's home. He had set up camp on a pestilential brown couch in the middle of the room, at the end of which he kept a paper bag containing most of his worldly possessions.

Everyone had gone to bed or passed out or fled into the night. In the absence of other ears to perplex and dazzle, Neal went to the music room, covered his own with headphones, put on some be-bop, and became it, dancing and doodley-oooping a Capella to a track I couldn't hear. While so engaged, he juggled the 36 oz. machinist's hammer which had become his trademark. The articulated jerky of his upper body ran monsoons of sweat and the hammer became a lethal blur floating in the air before him.

While the God's Amphetamine Cowboy spun, juggled and yelped joyous "doo-WOP's", Weir lay on his couch in the foreground, perfectly still, open eyes staring at the ceiling. There was something about the fixity of Bobby's gaze which seemed to indicate a fury of cognitive processing to match Neal's performance. It was as though Bobby were imagining him and going rigid with the effort involved in projecting such a tangible and kinetic image.

I also have a vague recollection of driving someplace in San Francisco with Neal and a amazingly lascivious redhead, but the combination of drugs and terror at his driving style has fuzzed this memory into a dreamish haze. I remember that the car was a large convertible, possibly a Cadillac, made in America at a time we still made cars of genuine steel but that its bulk didn't

18

seem like armor enough against a world coming at me so fast and close.

Nevertheless, I recall taking comfort in the notion that to have lived so long this way Cassady was probably invulnerable and that, if that were so, I was also within the aura of his mysterious protection.

Turned out I was wrong about that. About five months later, four days short of his 42nd birthday, he was found dead next to a railroad track outside San Miguel D'Allende, Mexico. He wandered out there in an altered state and died of exposure in the high desert night. Exposure seemed right. He had lived an exposed life. By then, it was beginning to feel like we all had.

In necessary dualities, there are only protagonists. The other protagonist of this song is Cassidy Law, who is now, in the summer of 1990, a beautiful and self-possessed young woman of 20.

When I first met her, she was less than a month old. She had just entered the world on the Rucka Rucka Ranch, a dust-pit of a one-horse ranch in the Nicasio Valley of West Marin which Bobby inhabited along with a variable cast of real characters.

These included Cassidy's mother Eileen, a good woman who was then and is still the patron saint of the Deadheads, the wolf-like Rex Jackson, a Pendleton cowboy turned Grateful Dead roadie in whose memory the Grateful Dead's Rex Foundation is named, Frankie Weir, Bobby's ol' lady and the subject of the

19

A LITERARY GENERATION'S LEGACY

song Sugar Magnolia, Sonny Heard, a Pendleton bad ol' boy
who was also a GD roadie, and several others I can't recall.

There was also a hammer-headed Appaloosa stud, a vile goat,
and miscellaneous barnyard fowl which included a peacock so
psychotic and aggressive that they had to keep a 2 x 4 next to
the front door to ward off his attacks on folks leaving the house.
In a rural sort of way, it was a pretty tough neighborhood. The
herd of horses across the road actually became rabid and had to
be destroyed.

It was an appropriate place to enter the 70's, a time of bleak
exile for most former flower children. The Grateful Dead had
been part of a general Diaspora from the Haight as soon as the
Summer of Love festered into the Winter of Our Bad Craziness.
They had been strewn like jetsam across the further reaches of
Marin County and were now digging in to see what would
happen next.

The prognosis wasn't so great. 1968 had given us, in addition to
Cassady's death, the Chicago Riots and the election of Richard
Nixon. 1969 had been, as Ken Kesey called it, "the year of the
downer", which described not only a new cultural preference for
stupid pills but also the sort of year which could mete out
Manson, Chappaquiddick, and Altamont in less than 6 weeks.

I was at loose ends myself. I'd written a novel, on the strength of
whose first half Farrar, Straus, & Giroux had given me a healthy
advance with which I was to write the second half. Instead, I
took the money and went to India, returning seven months later

a completely different guy. I spent the first 8 months of 1970 living in New York City and wrestling the damned thing to an ill-fitting conclusion, before tossing the results over a transom at Farrar, Straus, buying a new motorcycle to replace the one I'd just run into a stationary car at 85 mph, and heading to California.

It was a journey straight out of *Easy Rider*. I had a no-necked barbarian in a Dodge Super Bee try to run me off the road in New Jersey (for about 20 high speed miles) and was served, in my own Wyoming, a raw, skinned-out lamb's head with eyes still in it. I can still hear the dark laughter that chased me out of that restaurant.

Thus, by the time I got to the Rucka Rucka, I was in the right raw mood for the place. I remember two bright things glistening against this dreary backdrop. One was Eileen holding her beautiful baby girl, a catch-colt (as we used to call foals born out of pedigree) of Rex Jackson's.

And there were the chords which Bobby had strung together the night she was born, music which eventually be joined with these words to make the song Cassidy. He played them for me. Crouched on the bare boards of the kitchen floor in the late afternoon sun, he whanged out chords that rang like the bells of hell.

And rang in my head for the next two years, during which time I quit New York and, to my great surprise, became a rancher in Wyoming, thus beginning my own rural exile.

A LITERARY GENERATION'S LEGACY

In 1972, Bobby decided he wanted to make the solo album which became *Ace*. When he entered the studio in early February, he brought an odd lot of material, most of it germinative. We had spent some of January in my isolated Wyoming cabin working on songs but I don't believe we'd actually finished anything. I'd come up with some lyrics (for "Looks Like Rain" and most of "Black-Hearted Wind"). He worked out the full musical structure for Cassidy, but I still hadn't written any words for it.

Most of our time was passed drinking Wild Turkey, speculating grandly, and fighting both a series of magnificent blizzards and the house ghost (or whatever it was) which took particular delight in devilling both Weir and his Malamute dog.

(I went in one morning to wake Bobby and was astonished when he reared out of bed wearing what appeared to be black-face. He looked ready to burst into Sewanee River. Turned out the ghost had been at him. He'd placed at 3 AM call to the Shoshone shaman Rolling Thunder, who'd advised him that a quick and dirty ghost repellant was charcoal on the face. So he'd burned an entire box of Ohio Blue Tips and applied the results.)

I was still wrestling with the angel of Cassidy when he went back to California to start recording basic tracks. I knew some of what it was about ... the connection with Cassidy Law's birth was too direct to ignore ... but the rest of it evaded me. I told him that I'd join him in the studio and write it there.

Then my father began to die. He went into the hospital in Salt Lake City and I stayed on the ranch feeding cows and keeping the feed trails open with an ancient Allis-Chalmers bulldozer. The snow was three and a half feet deep on the level and blown into concrete castles around the haystacks.

Bobby was anxious for me to join him in California, but between the hardest winter in ten years and my father's diminishing future, I couldn't see how I was going to do it. I told him I'd try to complete the unfinished songs, "Cassidy" among them, at a distance.

On the 18th of February, I was told that my father's demise was imminent and that I would have to get to Salt Lake. Before I could get away, however, I would have to plow snow from enough stackyards to feed the herd for however long I might be gone. I fired up the bulldozer in a dawn so cold it seemed the air might break. I spent a long day in a cloud of whirling ice crystals, hypnotized by the steady 2600 rpm howl of its engine, and, sometime in the afternoon, the repeating chords of "Cassidy".

I thought a lot about my father and what we were and had been to one another. I thought about delicately balanced dance of necessary dualities. And for some reason, I started thinking about Neal, four years dead and still charging around America on the hot wheels of legend.

Somewhere in there, the words to "Cassidy" arrived, complete and intact. I just found myself singing the song as though I'd known it for years.

A LITERARY GENERATION'S LEGACY

I clanked back to my cabin in the gathering dusk. Alan Trist, an old friend of Bob Hunter's and a new friend of mine, was visiting. He'd been waiting for me there all day. Anxious to depart, I sent him out to nail wind-chinking on the horse barn while I typed up these words and packed. By nightfall, another great storm had arrived. We set out for Salt Lake in it, hoping to arrive there in time to close, one last time, the dark years between me and my father.

Grateful Dead songs are alive. Like other living things, they grow and metamorphose over time. Their music changes a little every time they're played. The words, avidly interpreted and reinterpreted by generations of Deadheads, become accretions of meaning and cultural flavor rather than static assertions of intent. By now, the Deadheads have written this song to a greater extent than I ever did.

The context changes and thus, everything in it. What "Cassidy" meant to an audience, many of whom had actually known Neal personally, is quite different from what it means to an audience which has largely never heard of the guy.

Some things don't change. People die. Others get born to take their place. Storms cover the land with trouble. And then, always, the sun breaks through again.

MY AUDITION FOR *ON THE ROAD*

by Levi Asher

New York Magazine said Francis Ford Coppola was holding an open casting call for all major parts in his upcoming film of *On The Road*. I thought: cool! I'm not nearly extroverted enough to play Dean Moriarty, but I could handle being Sal Paradise. I kinda look like my mental image of Sal – well hey, he's fictional, anybody can look like him if they want.

The article gave a date (Saturday, February 4th) and a location (St. Paul's Church on 58th and Columbus). I called the church for more information and was told to just show up at noon. Sounded easy enough ... but on Friday (one day before the casting call) I saw a poster around Greenwich Village that gave the real instructions. To try out, I'd have to bring an 8x10 photograph and a cassette tape (non-returnable) containing a one-minute reading from a long list of beat-related writers: Kerouac, Wolfe, Melville, Dos Passos, Proust, Rimbaud, Ginsberg, Spengler, Burroughs, etc.

I have absolutely no acting experience, and I haven't the slightest idea how to read onto a tape in an "actor-ly" fashion. What the fuck, I decided. I'll wing it. First I called my sister Sharon, who wanted to go to the audition with me. Sharon's really into Kerouac – in fact she was the one who persuaded me to read him for the first time. I told her about the 8x10 and the

25

cassette tape and her reaction was the same as mine: oh shit. But she agreed to do it.

I decided to read a section from the first part of *On The Road*, the passage where Sal and his friend Eddie pass through Shelton, Nebraska. First I tried to get myself into a Kerouac frame-of-mind – which means I got a little buzzed and paced around the bedroom scratching my head for a few minutes. Then I hit the record button and read the two paragraphs straight through, no planning and no rehearsing. Turned it off and, Kerouac-style, declared it a final draft – no revisions or second thoughts allowed. I took it into the living room and played it for my wife, who said it wasn't as bad as she thought it would be. Praise! Yes!

Neither Sharon nor I had 8x10's, but like any good Webmaster I have my trusty handheld photo scanner. I scanned a photo of Sharon 'on the road' – her then-boyfriend/now-husband Jeff took it during a cross-country trip.

For myself, I chose a photo taken on the roof of 206 E. 7th Street, the apartment building where Kerouac and Ginsberg and Burroughs took some famous photos of each other (someday I'll write a page about the photos I took there). I thought my picture might capture someone's attention because it was modeled after a well-known Ginsberg photo taken forty years earlier from the same roof.

I blew the scans up to full-page size and printed them on my HP DeskJet. Not exactly the finest quality, but hey we're talking Beat here.

Saturday morning I picked Sharon up at her place on the Upper West Side, and we listened to each other's tapes. She'd gone through several books looking for a good female bit to read, and settled on a letter Mardou Fox wrote to Leo Percepied in *Subterraneans*. Her husband Jeff got inspired and played a jazz record (Dizzy Gillespie) in the background, and Sharon and Jeff were both really excited about the tape because there was a certain horn bit that coincided perfectly with the moment where Sharon/Mardou read the word "Oh ..." – in fact they were so enamored of the tape they weren't sure they wanted to give it up, and we couldn't leave for the audition until they made a copy for them to keep. Sharon's tape didn't look exactly professional – she hadn't had a blank tape around, and just taped over a cassette of some female folksinger, Holly or Molly something ... I wondered what Coppola would think of me and Sharon, with our inkjet photographs and taped-over tapes.

It hadn't occurred to me yet that Coppola might not want to pay a real lot of attention to Sharon or me. I'm stupid this way: I always underestimate how many people will be interested in things I'm interested in. I was expecting to find maybe 30 or 40 people there; I figured I'd get to bullshit with Coppola and tell him how much I liked *The Godfather* and suggest a few camera angles for his scenes with Sal and Dean ... in short, I didn't have a clue. Because Sharon and I got there and there was a line of FIVE THOUSAND FUCKING PEOPLE STANDING IN THE

A LITERARY GENERATION'S LEGACY

FREEZING COLD OUTSIDE THE CHURCH BITCHING ABOUT HOW LONG THEY'D BEEN WAITING.

I'm not exaggerating about the number of people. I had no idea how many desperate actors there were in New York City. The church was on a long city block, and the line wound past the corner, all the way down the long end of the block, into a parking garage (because it was cold), back out of the parking garage, then around to the far corner and halfway down the block again. I'm not talking single-file either – the line was four or five people deep.

I'd been expecting a lot of bookish beatnik/hippie types (like me) to show up, but the crowd was largely made up of professional or semi-professional actors, and they didn't seem particularly interested in or knowledgeable about the Beats. They were mostly attractive and young, short-haired and neatly dressed, and many of them carried glossy 8x10 headshots. Sharon and I started talking to the people around us, mainly to three people:

- a 25-year-old brown-haired guy with a grunge-rock look. Had read a few pages of *On The Road* and hated it: "What was all that about dingledodies and burn, burn, burn ...?" His grunge look was deceptive – he was rehearsing for an off-broadway play about Kurt Cobain, and had grown his hair for the part. He showed me his photo and I was surprised: he had the clean-cut conventional appearance of any male lead in a soap opera.

- 19-year-old NYU student, female, who hadn't brought a tape or a picture. Never read Kerouac, perhaps never even heard of Kerouac. Had done some acting. Had a sort of cute 50's look and could have played Marylou, Dean's first wife. Kept talking about how terrible she looked today, maybe hoping somebody would contradict her.

- 46-year-old slightly batty woman, extensive and mostly unsuccessful acting experience. She and the pseudo-grunge guy found they knew a lot of the same industry people. Talked a lot. About five feet tall and slightly overweight. She had read some Kerouac, and I asked her what part she had in mind for herself. She said "I don't know, Camille?" which is Dean's beautiful 20-year-old second wife. Uh ... yeah. I guess you develop a really good imagination after a few years in this business.

There were many others, and we all got to know each other real well because we spent FOUR FUCKING HOURS standing out there. It was freezing cold, but in a way our mutual suffering brought us all together, and by the end of the wait we all knew everything about each other. It was kind of like *A Chorus Line* where we each take turns telling our life stories, except we didn't sing (well, one person did – actors are so hammy).

Sharon had to go home after a couple hours (she just had her first baby recently), but I was determined to make it inside. The line moved slowly. We entertained ourselves with jokes, coordinated jumping, coffee, cigarettes (I had three and I don't smoke). It was all kind of fun, although my toes got frozen stiff. The pseudo-grunge guy and the girl from NYU were looking kinda chummy by the fourth hour. I wonder if she'll still like him after he turns back into a soap star.

We got in the door at six-thirty (we'd arrived at two). They herded us into a basement auditorium in groups of three hundred, and passed us little pink slips of paper to write our personal statistics on. One of Coppola's assistants explained that they'd be letting us up to the front one bunch at a time, and all we were to do was hand in our slips, tapes and photos and say hello to Mr. Coppola. They told us to please not shake Mr. Coppola's hand, as he has a sore shoulder. What about auditioning? we all wondered. There was no audition, it turned out. We were to hand in our materials and let them look at us, and that was it. Perhaps they would make some sort of unspoken selection, but it was not clear how they would do this. After the long cold wait, we were all a bit stunned and didn't know what to think of this. The actors were more annoyed than I was, since I was really there just for fun (for them it was business).

My bunch went up. I handed in my tape and photo and slip, then moved on to the table where Francis Ford Coppola was greeting everybody. I spotted Allen Ginsberg sitting behind Coppola (I had a feeling he'd be there) and I thought of going up and speaking to him, but he looked tired, possibly even asleep behind those plastic goggle-glasses, and I decided not to bother him. Coppola seemed to be in a very good mood. Somebody handed him a trumpet (I don't know what the significance of this is) and he played a few notes. I was surprised how jovial, almost goofy, he looked. He actually resembles Allen Ginsberg, except that he's younger and much heavier, so it was strange to see them both together in the same place.

I happen to like Coppola a lot (he directed the *Godfather* films, *Apocalypse Now* and *The Outsiders*, in case you didn't know), and I was kind of excited to meet him. When it was my turn he actually reached out and shook my hand, which surprised me because we'd been told that handshakes were a no-no. He had BIG beefy hands. I said, "I hope you'll make a great film" and he said "Yeah, well, we've got to get started", or something like that. It was hard to concentrate with all the other actors clamoring behind me. I moved on.

Well, that's the story of my first cattle-call. It's been five days and nobody's called me back yet. If I get called I'll let you all know. But I feel kinda 'Hollywood' now anyway, just from the experience of hanging out with all those actors for a whole day. So ta-ta for now (*kiss, kiss*). And I'd like to thank ... ah fuck it.

A LITERARY GENERATION'S LEGACY

RINGSIDE SEAT: GERALD NICOSIA vs. ANN CHARTERS AT N.Y.U.

by Levi Asher

The "Writings of Jack Kerouac" conference at New York University began on June 4, 1995 as scheduled – and that was about the last thing that went the way it was supposed to. The first sign that events were spinning in several orbits outside the control of the event orgaziners came a few days before it began when the Unbearables, an inspired and largely disorganized group of angry downtown writers announced a counter-gathering to protest the complacency and dullness of the NYU event. They would host a series of alternative events, including a Jack Kerouac Impersonators Spontaneous Prose contest, to take place around New York City at the same time as the official events.

The Unbearables announcement immediately began drawing more attention (in the *Village Voice*, for instance, and on my own website) than the official conference announcement. I exchanged emails with a few of these Unbearables, and promptly decided to cast my lot with them. I wasn't sure how much they would have to say, but at least this was going to be something *new*, and the Unbearables weren't planning to lighten my wallet by $140 for "registration" either. Also, panel discussions bore me and I hate wearing "HELLO! My Name Is ..." tags. Easy decision.

32

The Unbearables' protest, though, ended up being upstaged by a much more shocking one. The fate of Jack Kerouac's estate and legacy has been a topic of controversy for some time now; the Sampas family (Kerouac's last wife was Stella Sampas) owns everything, basically, and Jack's daughter Jan has been vying for a share. Jan Kerouac was barely recognized as a daughter by Jack during his lifetime, and her attempts at being included in the "family" now have mostly been rebuffed. Jan (author of a couple of books, including *Baby Driver*, which I heard was pretty good) has also been very sick with kidney failure lately, and the fact of her illness must be contributing to the general intensity of feeling regarding the controversy of her involvement in the ownership of her father's estate.

That's enough background – now I'll get to the fireworks. Gerald Nicosia, author of the most acclaimed major Kerouac biography, *Memory Babe*, was apparently not invited to participate in any part of the NYU conference. Ann Charters, who had authored the first major Kerouac biography *Kerouac* in 1973, was invited. Because Ann Charters has been considered 'friendly' by the Sampas family while Nicosia has expressed support for Jan Kerouac, Nicosia believes that his exclusion from the conference was a conspiracy against himself and Jan.

This may very well be the case. But get this: Nicosia showed up at the conference anyway, wearing a black t-shirt that said

"Gerald Nicosia ...
A tiresome wannabe"

33

A LITERARY GENERATION'S LEGACY

– Ann Charters

on the front. On the back were pictures of Jan and some member of the Sampas family (I didn't get a good enough look), and, in rock-concert style bold colorful print, the words "KEROUAC VS. SAMPAS". He also wore his "HELLO! My Name Is ..." tag upside down, and had replaced the words "Kerouac Conference" with "Sampas Conference."

I found his confrontational approach very surprising. Nicosia is quite an established figure in the Kerouac 'field,' and I've heard people praise his book – the longest and most thorough as well as the most recent of all the Kerouac biographies – more than any other, including Charters'. He was certainly risking his reputation by airing his grievances in such a public fashion.

It is admirable, I suppose, that he is doing this not for himself, but for Jan Kerouac. At the same time, as I watched Nicosia wander the lobby outside the auditorium where booksellers and Kerouac-interest-groups had set up tables and where people like me (who hadn't paid to get in) hung around taking in the scenery, I detected a certain psychotic intensity to the expression on his face, and it occurred to me that he was maybe taking this all a little *too* seriously.

This opinion was reinforced when I talked to some other people hanging out around the lobby. I heard that somebody – either a Jan/Nicosia supporter, or Nicosia himself – had disrupted one of the conferences in the morning. Later I was talking to someone else about the Beat figures who were hanging around the lobby

34

(at that moment, Anne Waldman, Joyce Johnson and Ray Bremser as well as Nicosia) and this person was telling me about the conversations he'd had with them. He looked at Nicosia and advised me, "Don't talk to him unless you want to do a lot of listening."

That was Act One: Act Two took place at Biblio's bookstore in Tribeca, where the Unbearables were staging their Jack Kerouac Impersonators Contest. Ann Charters showed up with her husband Sam (a legendary blues author, who wrote *Country Blues* and *The Blues Makers*, and who played a very important part in the late-fifties/early-sixties rediscovery of Robert Johnson, Son House and many other old bluesmen). They were sitting at a table with a very nice guy named Ralph, from Minneapolis, who I'd recently talked to in the NYU lobby. Ralph offered me a seat near him, and so I suddenly found myself sitting next to Ann and Sam Charters. *Then* in comes Gerald Nicosia, still wearing his black t-shirt with the nasty Ann Charters quotation on the front, and he heads straight for our table. Ann sees him coming and looks away.

"Excuse me, Ann", Gerald Nicosia says. "I just had to ask you ... do you think it's right that I was forcibly removed from the conference this morning under threat of police intervention?"

Or something like that. Ann tries to play it cool. "I know nothing about it, Gerald. I had a cold today, and wasn't even at the conference."

A LITERARY GENERATION'S LEGACY

"Well, do you think it was right? And do you think it's right that so-and-so Jan Kerouac-this and Sampas-family that and so-on and so-forth ..." all in a strident, nearly-threatening tone of voice. He does not seem far from physical violence, although this would not have been much of a problem, as Sam Charters is about a foot taller and a hundred pounds heavier than Nicosia. Ann keeps trying to put off his questions. "I'm very sorry that happened, Gerald" "I really don't know what it is you want me to do about that" and so on. Nicosia finally walks away, simmers for a few minutes, then comes back even angrier, and starts in again.

All the time I'm sitting there thinking: Wow. I'm sitting here watching the two major Kerouac biographers duke it out, and I've got a ringside seat.

I'm now going to do something I've never done before in Literary Kicks. I've never expressed my opinion on the Jan vs. Sampas Family hijinks, and that's mainly because I think the whole thing is kind of dumb. I also don't think it's very interesting to serious Kerouac readers – although from my seat at Biblio's I have to admit it was starting to get pretty damn interesting.

Anywhere, here's how I call it, for what it's worth:

- Every family has problems, and there is nothing surprising about the fact that Jan Kerouac (Jack's daughter from his second marriage, and a daughter that he refused to recognize and almost never met) is not friendly with the family of Jack's last wife. I'm not saying the Sampas family is right to snub her, or that she should not feel free to express how she feels about being snubbed. But like I said, every family has problems, and I don't see why this particular problem (which is all about money, really, and has nothing to do with incest or rape or death or drugs or anything like that) should be blown up into such a major public issue.

- Jan Kerouac and Gerald Nicosia are saying that the Sampas family is getting rich by selling off the Kerouac papers little by little, and that they should instead donate or sell the entire Kerouac archive to a library. Well ... okay, whatever. My problem with this argument is: who really cares? Maybe it's better for a single library to own the whole thing, but is this really a critical issue?

You all know how much I care about Kerouac's life and work. But let's admit it ... the guy published enough stuff even during his lifetime to keep his readers busy for years, even decades. And that's not to mention his voluminous letters and journals and art notebooks, and the reminiscences of his many friends and lovers and compatriots. If you put me in a room with the entire Kerouac archive right now, I don't honestly know how interested I'd be. I haven't even gotten around to reading *Vanity of Duluoz* yet!

I always find it ridiculous when people make too big a deal over a writer's personal archive. No writer is *that* good. Kerouac was a man, not a holy savior. Just chill out, everybody, all right?

- By the end of the night I had spoken to Ann Charters, and I liked her. I'm aware that many serious students of Beat literature consider her to be a little too chummy with Allen Ginsberg and other major living Beat figures to be able to write objectively about them. She's been accused of prettying up some ugly truths about Jack Kerouac in her book. Her ethics have been challenged by Tim Bowden, who in the early 1970s observed her taking advantage of Carolyn Cassady to get material for her (he accuses Charters of bringing a friend to Carolyn's house to engage Carolyn in a vapid discussion while she furiously scribbles notes from Carolyn's personal papers).

  These things may or may not be true, but none of them seem like terrible offenses to me, and I'd like to say a word in her defense.

  This woman wrote about Jack Kerouac in 1973, back when *nobody* took him seriously as a writer. I mean, *NOBODY*. Her book wasn't even published by an established firm: Straight Arrow Books was a division of *Rolling Stone* magazine. That was what the mainstream literary world thought of Jack Kerouac back in '73, four years after his death. It took courage, vision and selfless dedication to devote her career to a a writer whose literary reputation had never been good, and was now in a state of utter ruin.

Now everybody from Viking Penguin to New York University kisses Kerouac's ass, and it's an all-new world for Beat scholarship. But let's have a little respect for the person who put her reputation on the line back when it meant something. Yeah, Nicosia is sticking up for Jan Kerouac. But Ann Charters once stuck up for Jack Kerouac, and that means something more.

Okay, I'm done talking about this. I'd like to conclude this report with a big "YEEE-HAHHH!" for the Unbearables, who put on a fun, truly spontaneous show at Biblio's. It started off with some jokes that were pretty dumb, focusing mainly on a burly guy in a mustache running around in a wig and housedress pretending to be Kerouac's mother. Kinda cute, kinda reminiscent of The Diggers, but also much too long. Some of the audience left during this part, but then the night started to get going, and a session of Kerouac-inspired spontaneous rants and readings began to really generate some steam. Some of it was even good writing, and almost all of it was good ranting. The Unbearables are a cool bunch; I've heard they've previously protested the bad poetry in the *New Yorker*, to which I can only say: what about the shitty fiction?

At one point during the Sip A Beer With Mrs. Kerouac Contest I leaned over to Ann Charters and said "You know, it just occurred to me that you're the only person in this room who actually *did* sip a beer with Mrs. Kerouac."

39

She replied, "It was actually champagne. She only drank champagne."

"Oh really?" I said. "Expensive stuff, or cheap?"

"Cheap stuff", Ann Charters said.

That's the end of my report. You'll notice I didn't say anything about the conferences themselves. They're still going on today, as I sit at home writing this up. I have a feeling I'm not missing much. As for what's going on in the lobby ... I think I've seen enough already.

JOHN MONTGOMERY, DHARMA BUM

by Jim Stedman

In my efforts to pull on the shirtsleeves of them that were left of the Beat Generation, I came across some works edited by one John McVey Montgomery, who (according to Ann Charters) appeared as the cameo character Henry Morley in Jack Kerouac's book *The Dharma Bums*. Morley was the clownish character who rambled through the Sierra bramble, accompanying Jack and Gary Snyder until realizing that he'd forgotten to drain the water from his auto's radiator. Morley turned back, heading down the trail and waving over his shoulder that he'd join his companions at a later tick of the clock, only to disappear.

John M. Montgomery edited a number of books about Kerouac, and I ordered these from the publisher, Fels and Firn, attaching a note to John on the order. As I suspected, Fels and Firn was John, and he was pleased to hear from me, pleased to receive a check, and pleased to engage in a correspondence that lasted for five years.

When I'd least expect it, I'd receive a postcard or letter from John, each one typed out in an odd font. He would respond to questions, ask questions of his own, or talk up the idea of having the library in Marquette, Michigan order his books and sponsor his coming to town to talk about Jack and, well, everything.

41

A LITERARY GENERATION'S LEGACY

At one point, I asked John what he thought about Jack Kerouac's attitude regarding the working class. His response was:

> *While Jack and I never talked about the working class, I don't think he thought of it as a political class. He wanted to go back to Cape Cod to live at the end and has got Memere to agree (sic) He never liked Florida and went there only as a trade with Memere when she agreed to try and regain her strength after her stroke, and was sore that she did not take physiotherapy or exercise. He also told Stella he planned to divorce her. I don't know why he moved to Hyannis or Northport but he went to bars where clammers went in Northport.*
>
> *I don't think Kerouac liked working at "jobs" thus I don't think there was any guilt regarding that. He thought of his writing as work but he was inconsistent also waiting for bursts of inspiration so that he would write long hours for several days trying to write a whole book. It was a negative thing about the workers. He distrusts people with money partly because of what he saw as a student at Horace Mann. I think it was inherited from his parents. He distrusted professors and was apprehensive when he had to make an appearance at Lowell House at Harvard. So that is he felt more comfortable with working, that is, uneducated people.*

Most of his reading with an idea of imitating as a writer was done in high school. He read and studied all his life but not particularly for literature. He read McLuhan in about 1965, for example. The Buddhist period meant heavy reading but then he ended it and went on. My ideas come from reading Kerouac's books. I think the 4 chaplains and the sinking of his ship, the Dorchester, might have given him some feeling of guilt but the main reason for the guilt was being brought up by nuns until he entered a different school for the fourth grade.

Kerouac did not feel guilt as to sex like many Catholics, but he did not want marriage. He was of course shocked to learn of Edie's abortion. Jack was friendly and loyal to his nephew Paul Jr., whom I met. Marriage would have meant that Kerouac would have had to reduce his nights in bars and at the homes of his men friends and he did not want to give that up. I think Kerouac was satisfied with his books though he did say that he could do no better than "Visions of Cody." He stood by his books and I do not think he recanted. He did tell me that "On The Road" and "The Dharma Bums" were potboilers and that he would not write any more potboilers.

He said it was truer to call himself Jack than John as he did in "Town and the City." Well, I don't claim to have all the answers but most of the writers about Kerouac are a bit twisted in my view. That's why my

A LITERARY GENERATION'S LEGACY

> *books on Jack are as far as possible writ by people*
> *who knew him and I did not edit them.*
> *(sales pitch deleted)*
> *Best, John Montgomery*

In the autumn of 1992, I received the following letter:

> *To the Friends of John Montgomery:*
>
> *My father, John Montgomery, died of a heart attack*
> *on Friday, June 5, 1992, at Kaiser Hospital in San*
> *Rafael. He had been hiking at Kent Lake in Marin*
> *when he had his first heart attack, and we had a*
> *week of visits together before he passed away from a*
> *second one. I found your name in his address book*
> *and thought you would like to know. I am asking*
> *those who knew him if they would write about how*
> *they were connected to him and a memory or two (an*
> *anecdote or whatever you wish to share with me) for*
> *a festschrift. If you would like a copy of this, please*
> *let me know and I would be happy to send you one.*
>
> *Memorial services were held privately by the family.*
>
> *Sincerely,*
> *Laura Montgomery Petersen*

I wrote back to John's daughter, explaining our connection, and
included a cryptic sort-of poem for the collection.

I found John to be a very loyal correspondent. Extremely witty and verbose and obviously cosmos-knowledgeable, John Montgomery was every bit the madman Jack described him to be.

My friend Tim Bowden, who became Carolyn Cassady's companion and knew many of the Beat writers during the early 1970s, has also written a few reminiscences of John Montgomery:

> I knew John Montgomery when I was living in Los Gatos with Carolyn Cassady. John had been led to believe by Lawrence Ferlinghetti that Carolyn might be available, so his trips to Los Gatos were a sort of courtship. He is somebody who stepped right out of his character in Dharma Bums – the vague and surrealistic Henry Morley muttering inanities all down the lonesome trail. Just like in Bums, he would show up with gifts pilfered from around the Goodwill drops in the night.
>
> Once he came with a Siamese cat. Did he remember we had a dog, Goofy? John didn't. His arm was shredded, and he wailed "Would you grab that dog, PLEASE?" while he went to retrieve his cat from the back of the house. John left with the Siamese, arm bleeding, and never mentioned it again.
>
> John was making the rounds of friends with typewriters. He had an idea for a manuscript which was enhanced by Carolyn's connection with Rolling Stone magazine and Straight Arrow

45

Books. He wondered if she might interest them in his work. She offered no enthusiasm.

In the days before multiple fonts and word processors, John intended finding different type styles from the various typewriters he could locate. The idea was some sort of a dialogue, and I can only remember a scrap he read to me. One line referenced a literary lion, and the next column explained those sort were not often invited to the same lunch as those at the zoo. It was sort of a cracked wordplay game, near as I could figure.

Of all the brokendown heroes I encountered during these years, John was the most critical of Kerouac. He never could forgive his image as the doddering klutz on Matterhorn in Dharma Bums. I can remember tossing a softball ("Jack was quite a woodsman, ey?") and John slapping it away with a snarl, "No, he wasn't!".

A NOTE FROM LOS GATOS: THE JOHN CASSADY INTERVIEW

by Levi Asher

In August 1995, a few days after the death of Jerry Garcia, I received an email from a woman named Pat Gallagher, who lived in San Jose and had been perusing Literary Kicks with "my friend, John Cassady". It was lucky that I happened to read this email carefully, or I might have missed the hidden bombshell.

John who? I knew that Neal Cassady had several children before he died in 1968, and I remembered Jack Kerouac's description of little white-haired "Timmy Pomeroy", a cheerful Cassady kid, in the novels *Big Sur* and *Visions of Cody*. But I had no idea where any of Neal's children were today, or how they were faring. Pat Gallagher's introductory email gave me a chance to publish the first interview with John Cassady, who was working as a support analyst for a Silicon Valley technology company and still living in the Los Gatos house that had once been Neal and Carolyn's home. John, it turned out, was ready to start talking, and I had plenty of questions to ask. The following published interview was assembled from a long transcript of email conversations.

Levi: So what have you been up to lately? Where do you work, what do you do for fun, etc.?

47

A LITERARY GENERATION'S LEGACY

John: Let's start at the beginning. First, the Earth cooled ...

No, we'll skip to my birth in San Francisco, September 9, 1951. By about age three we had settled in Los Gatos, a small town in the foothills 50 miles south of San Francisco, which I've gravitated back to ever since. While living in the coastal resort town of Santa Cruz for most of the '70s, what I lacked in career motivation I made up for in life experience and having fun. Along the way I harvested a son, Jamie Neal, born August 18, 1975, who still lives with me while attending a local community college, and I also tried my hand at marriage on two occasions in different decades.

I moved back to Los Gatos and Silicon Valley in 1983 to pursue a career in (what else?) electronics and computers. The field wasn't my first choice, preferring to play guitar in rock bands, but, as they say, "when in Rome." My music career certainly couldn't be counted upon to pay the bills. So I've been fairly settled since then, having lived in the same house in south San Jose for the past seven years.

My '90s lifestyle is much more stable and less crazy than in years past. For the past 12 years I've been with Caere Corporation, producer of page-reading software and scanner systems, in (where else?) Los Gatos. It's a good gig and I'm reasonably comfortable.

And for fun? Sorry, no time. Actually, I like to hang out with my girlfriend Pat and read, watch flicks or whatnot. Occasionally I'll dust off the guitars to play with friends at open mike nights or recording sessions. Then there's always the unabashed self-promotion on the Net! (This is my first, honest). So that about sums it up in one, long paragraph. Pretty frigging boring, eh?

Levi: Tell me more about your music.

John: I listened to KEWB, Channel 91, out of San Francisco as a little kid. I dug stuff like Bobby Darin's "Splish Splash" and all the novelty songs like "The Flying Purple People Eater" and "Monster Mash." Everything by Ray Stevens and the Coasters. My parents were into cool jazz, of course, which was a great influence later. "Sketches of Spain" by Miles is permanently imprinted in my brain, after so many nights falling asleep to that album drifting in from the party in the living room.

At age 13, three pals and I bought Beatle wigs, put up posters around the neighborhood, and put on a "show." We set up a picnic table with Hi-fi speakers hidden underneath, and actually climbed up there and played tennis rackets (and a wash tub) while lip synching to the Beatles "Second Album". Dweeb city. The girls loved us. I had found my calling.

I met a blues-harp player in college, an ex-Marine just out of Vietnam named Matt Shaw. He learned blues harp by hiding in the ammo bunker under his fire base near Laos and playing Paul Butterfield's classic "East/West" album over and over. What a killer harmonica player Matt was by the time I met him. He lived in a little house out in the middle of this huge orchard where we made big noise without complaints.

A LITERARY GENERATION'S LEGACY

We got pretty good and eventually quit college and moved to a little town called Felton in the San Lorenzo Valley of the Santa Cruz Mountains, surrounded by redwood trees and hippies. We named our new band The Feltones. Actually, "Those" Fabulous Feltones is what we decided on because it had a more notorious ring to it. And notorious we were. The drummer was a madman. Triple Scorpio coke dealer; need I say more? The girls loved him. He even stole my old lady for a while, but we were all friends. We played venues like the Catalyst in Santa Cruz, the Chateau Liberte and the Town & Country Lodge in Ben Lomond, all legendary bars back when SC was wild. I could write volumes. Someday I will. "The Adventures of The Fabulous Feltones."

Levi: What were some of your favorite Grateful Dead songs?

John: I saw them a lot in the '60s, and then our paths didn't cross for many years, so I missed most of their later albums. In fact, I couldn't win any trivia contests after "American Beauty", although I listened to "Europe '72" quite a bit at the time. I loved their first album, and figured out every Dexedrine-propelled Jerry lick on it that I could as a wanna-be guitarist. "Viola Lee Blues", etc. I loved Pig Pen's version of "Love Light." We'd stand under him stoned at the Avalon Ballroom in SF and not even notice that he'd drag it out to 45 minutes sometimes. Every track on "Workingman's Dead." Of course "Casey Jones." "Dire Wolf" especially reminds me of Jerry now (since August 9th). Dead standards like "Ripple", "Birdsong" and many I can't recall right now are great. I leaned toward the Garcia/Hunter compositions.

Levi: Tell me about your son.

John: I'm a single parent with my twenty-year-old son living with me. I've been married and divorced twice. Pat and I have been an item for exactly one year now, the proverbial office romance. My son's name is Jamie, named for one of my sisters, and he is working and attending a local community college. He turned out pretty good, although I don't see much of him. He and his girlfriend come up for air every few days and I catch sight of him then. I was going to name him Cody, after the character Pomerey in Jack's *Visions of*. His middle name is Neal.

Levi: Do you get a lot of recognition in your everyday life for being Neal's son?

John: Naw. There's always been the occasional letter or call.

Levi: Has the interest increased recently, or not? And does it bug you?

John: I love it. Who else gets to garner attention and strokes for something they had nothing whatsoever to do with? The only thing that's a little scary is having to carry the torch someday. My mother's got so many stories and knowledge that hasn't been shared. I don't think I can adequately represent the legend with authority, so most of the good stuff will be lost with her passing.

Levi: I've bragged to all my friends about getting e-mail from you already –

A LITERARY GENERATION'S LEGACY

John: … cool!

Levi: – but I'm keeping your email address to myself, or else god knows what kind of weirdos you'd start hearing from (and that's just my friends ...)

But it must be a funny thing being Neal Cassady's son, because while he is so well-known and beloved in some circles, I would guess that most people in America have never heard of him. Just how much has being 'Neal's son' colored your identity in life?

John: Being the son of an infamous "legend" is a constant source of surprise, amazement and pride. Surprise and amazement because, to this day, I can't believe how many people *have* heard of him. Pride because, although I had nothing to do with the legend's conception, I agree with those that regard the man as something special on this planet. Of course, my perspective is somewhat biased, having loved him as a father as well as a hip icon. I feel fortunate that I was in the unique position to do both.

I've been blessed with the opportunity to meet so many fascinating individuals who operate on levels of art and wisdom that I admire and to which I long to aspire. Doors of opportunity have been opened, most of which I haven't taken advantage of, I guess for fear of exploiting something intangible that I don't think is mine to abuse. But the outpouring of friends and fans has always been a pleasant surprise over the years and is something I still think is great.

Levi: Beat aficionados like me have heard 'visions of Neal' from many people – Jack Kerouac (of course), Allen Ginsberg, Ken Kesey, Charles Bukowski, John Perry Barlow, your mother, etc. How about your visions – can you give us a memory or two we haven't heard before?

John: By far the number one question asked re: Neal is: "Did you ever know/see/remember your father?" And a good question it is, too, because he was everywhere else at once. The more I learn about his life from other sources, the more I'm amazed that I ever did see him, much less how much. It's simply astounding. He really was everywhere at the same time. How he pulled it off, we'll never know.

To me he was Dad, although admittedly he was absent more than I would have liked. But my memories are almost as plentiful as if I had been brought up by "normal" parents.

Levi: What was it like being a kid in the back seat with "the fastest man alive" behind the wheel?

John: Those are images I'll never forget. On Friday nights he would take me, and sometimes one or two of my best buddies, to the quarter-mile oval race track called San Jose Speedway out in the dusty fields about 10 miles from our home in Los Gatos. Driving there and back was most of the adventure, especially on the return trip, after he'd watch his heroes slide the midget racers sideways around the track all night. I can still smell the tire dust and fuel fumes that would drive Dad into a

53

frenzy. He'd get so excited that he'd elbow me in the ribs and point till I was bruised, but I loved every minute of it. Of course, at the age of 10 or so, I was usually more interested in crawling around under the bleachers or going for an ice cream sandwich. I was always getting lost, especially when my friends came along.

While driving, he was fond of jerking the steering wheel to the beat of the rock and roll on the car radio. Chuck Berry was one of his favorites, and songs like "Maybelline" and "Nadine" fit him to a T. Two pals and I would be in the back seat and knock heads every time he jerked the car onto two wheels side to side going down the freeway, and we'd giggle uncontrollably and hold our sides. My friends thought he was about the coolest dad on the planet. Their parents probably didn't agree.

There was a guy named Roy who owned Los Gatos Tire Service who gave Dad a job when no one else would after he was released from San Quentin. Neal had the drug rap on his record which was, in 1960, tantamount to being an ax murderer. No one asked if he'd been sent up for two sticks of tea. Old Roy could have cared less.

Roy was known to have a drink or two, and died sometime in the '70s, but not before repeating some of his favorite Neal stories to a young man who worked there starting in about '72. I ran into this guy by coincidence when I had some tire work done at the present location of the shop, and after seeing my last name on the work order, he was glad to share some of Roy's stories with me. Roy's favorite was how Neal would drive his car down from our house, which was two miles up a hill from the tire shop, without the benefit of brakes, an almost obsessive pastime of Dad's. I believe this would have been the '49 Pontiac. Anyway, he would time it perfectly every morning so the car would bump up into the driveway (after having slowed it by rubbing curbs when necessary), he would then hop out in front of the garage doors, and the car would continue along the flat driveway, the door flapping shut, and on out to the back dirt parking lot, where it would nudge over a small mound so the front wheels would rock back and forth to settle into the dirt trough beyond. It never failed to amaze and delight Roy.

Another amazing story, which I can't verify but is great, has it that one night Roy passed Neal going the other way through town and waved. Neal threw the car into reverse and caught up with Roy, the transmission screaming, and chatted with him door to door while driving backwards, glancing back occasionally for oncoming traffic. Dad had a penchant for driving in reverse, probably because the steering is so squirrely, like driving a fork lift. He was proud of his downhill-in-reverse speed record on Lombard Street, the twisty tourist trap in San Francisco.

Levi: You were Jack Kerouac's godson, and there are several references to you and your sisters in the Kerouac/Cassady letters. What do you remember of him?

John: My memories of Jack are few and sketchy; mostly just images of him rather than conversations. My sisters would remember more. The images are hazy from when he was around a lot at the new Los Gatos house because I was under five.

I better recall being around age ten and going to Big Sur when he was living in Lawrence Ferlinghetti's cabin in Bixby Canyon, driving down in Dad's new (to us) Willys jeep wagon, what a ride! Jack took time to instruct me on the nuances of packing a proper rucksack and keeping my socks dry. I confused him with Jack London when he was in his plaid-wool-shirt-in-the-woods phase. We would wander down the creek trail to the beach and stand in front of the immense surf which seemed to tower over us like a wall of water as in *The Ten Commandments*. He would yell into the din with arms outstretched; I'd explore an old wrecked car resting on its top at the foot of the cliff, looking for skeletons. I had no idea he was loaded on wine and/or pot the whole time, and wouldn't have cared less.

He was funny and kind and gentle and took a goofy interest in our kid stuff that parents might find tedious. At least that's my impression after all these years.

Ginsberg, of course, was around a lot more in years to come, and I still see him whenever possible.

Levi: What was the first Kerouac book that you read? What did you think of it, and what do you think of him as a writer now?

John: I first read *On the Road* at about age 15. I dug it but forgot most of it until just this year when I read it again and really enjoyed it. I also read *Dharma Bums* as a teenager and thought it pretty good, but I was never much of a reader, being too busy goofing off, which I now regret. I made a stab at the rest of Jack's stuff and couldn't make sense of it. I frankly think it reads like drunken ramblings that one must struggle to comprehend. Such blasphemy from his Godson!

Levi: Was it obvious to you as a child that Jack had romantic feelings for your mother?

John: I had no clue about an intimate relationship between Jack and my mom until I was grown. By that time I thought it was far out, to use the vernacular of the times. I was a baby when all this was going on, but I think Jack always carried the torch. Toward the end, he would call at like 3:00 a.m. drunk and ramble and rave, my mom trying to politely get him off the phone. I answered one night and only vaguely remember him crying "Johnny!" and "I have to speak to Carolyn!" I handed her the phone with a "whoa!" as she looked worried. We were more sad than surprised upon his demise.

(I asked John about the new Coppola movie of *On The Road*, and this led to a discussion of a previous, less-than-satisfying attempt at translating the Kerouac/Cassady legend onto film. *Heart Beat,* starring Nick Nolte and Sissy Spacek, was based on the book of the same title by John's mother, Carolyn Cassady. I mentioned that I'd never seen a copy of this book, though I'd read and enjoyed her later book, *Off The Road.*)

John: *Heart Beat* has been out of print for twenty years, so don't bother. It's actually only an excerpt of *Off the Road*, anyway. A publisher in Berkeley chopped the juicy chapters out of her original manuscript, the *menage a trois* parts, and sold that, a travesty taken out of context. Then, as you know, Orion picked up the movie rights and made an even worse film of it. Nick Nolte, I thought, wasn't as bad as the script and director. We were disgusted, especially since they promised some creative control.

Levi: But did you think Nick Nolte captured your father at all? Obviously you would know best ... as I said in my review of the movie in Literary Kicks, though, Nolte's schtick seems to be the surly, snarling kinda-deep-and-sad tough guy, which is not at all my image of your father.

John: An astute observation. Nolte's whole persona is the antithesis of Neal's. Every film Nick is in, that's Nick. He talks and acts the same off the set. He certainly tried hard on *Heart Beat*, though. He told me he had studied Neal a lot and based his previous movie's character on him. It was a war flick called *Who'll Stop the Rain?* Looked like Nick to me. The only time he came at all close in Heart Beat was the last scene when he calls Carolyn from the phone booth burned out. He sounded sad enough for that stage of life.

I flew down to watch them film, and fell in love with Sissy Spacek, what a doll she was. (Her husband agrees.) I was also very fond of Nick and his party materials, especially at the all-night wrap party at the Beverly Hills Hotel, where we hid at a corner table and blabbed for hours. We're both clean nowadays (this was 1977), but that was way fun. He wanted me to come up to his ranch in Malibu and ride dirt bikes and play some more, and like an idiot I declined and flew home, fool. I think I hurt his feelings. Never heard from him again. Well, we all have regrets. I just have more than others! I could write volumes.

Sissy also did her best to save the rotten script, and read the entire 1100-page manuscript of my mother's book to get into the role. Those two really hit it off, and during filming Sissy used the same approach with Loretta Lynn, studying for her next film, *Coal Miner's Daughter*. She's a pro. The thing about *Heart Beat* was they just bought the names and made up their own story, with just some highlights based in fact. John Byrum (writer/director) didn't do his homework and it showed. They could have made it authentic, almost a documentary, and still had all the stuff that sells: sex, drugs, violence, and it would have been the real thing. Stupid waste. My mother was so disappointed in the script that she wrote her own screenplay. Of course they didn't use it because they had already paid off Byrum. Oh well.

Levi: Who would be the ideal movie "Neal"?

John: The only actor I've seen that came close was Paul Newman in 1957's *Somebody Up There Likes Me*, the Rocky Marciano bio. When he wore a tight t-shirt and smiled, he was a dead ringer. Too bad he's too old for the part now. There are a couple unknowns that my mother likes.

(John told me about a business trip to Denver, the city where Neal grew up.)

59

A LITERARY GENERATION'S LEGACY

John: I flew to Denver on business and wound up on Larimer Street among the gloomy brick ruins of my father's past, hoping for a glimpse of the ghosts of little Neal and Neal Sr. down an alley off the dark street. We took some clients to a downtown restaurant for dinner, one of whom was a Kerouac fan, and my colleague and I took a wrong turn trying to find the freeway out of town and to the airport. Suddenly we were in the worst part of town, amid old abandoned buildings and railway depots, but with rickety wood houses, shops and bars wedged in-between, still occupied. Then there it was, Larimer Street, as well as several other street names familiar from *On the Road* and *The First Third*. Unlike the modern Larimer Square and other tourist traps up the road, this section didn't invite exploration that late at night, but I finally got to see it and get its feel, even from behind a rental car window. It was an unexpected treat.

Levi: Penguin sent me the new Kerouac CD-Rom last night (free stuff, about the only perk I get for doing Litkicks) and in the Gallery section I was pleased to see a photo of a bearded Neal surrounded by three nice-looking kids including a cute and pudgy tousle-haired tyke ... John, that was you!

John: I haven't seen this CD-Rom yet, although it's all I heard about for months from my mother while they were working on it. They solicited a lot of material from her, and she was enthusiastic about helping them because they seemed genuine and they paid well for pictures and stuff. But in the end they used only a fraction of the stuff she'd sent, a typical disappointment.

"Pops" grew the beard after one of his railroad accidents when he was home for months recuperating. If it's the picture I'm thinking of, I was only months old. That picture has been in several books. I was so "pudgy" (read: fat) that it looks like they have rubber bands around the joints on my arms and legs, and I'm puffing my cheeks out. There's a later one with beard in our back yard in San Jose where I'm about two and have a buzz cut on my massive head. So flattering.

Levi: Neal looks great in a beard – how the hell did he stay so fit? Did he ever eat? Did he work out? Somehow I can't picture him in a Soloflex, so it must have been his work and all that legendary hammer-flipping – but then I know a lot of people who do physical work, and they don't look so great.

John: He worked out on free weights a lot as a teenager, probably at reform school and in Denver skid row gyms. He was born with a great physique and developed it early. Later it was work that kept it tight, sprinting in parking lots, walking miles in the rail yards, tossing truck tires in and out of the retreader. He didn't start the hammer schtick until shortly before his death.

(One day John wrote me about an event in England.)

John: I called Mum Tuesday, October 17, to ask how the big poetry festival at the Albert Hall went the night before at which Ginsberg was supposed to perform. She said he called her that day and was really chummy but had declined comp tickets because it was a benefit (jeez), but luckily a couple of her fans

61

insisted on escorting her and bought seats at seventh row center. Allen comes out and after some "one-liners", one about Neal, he introduces his accompanist for the evening, a job I used to do on guitar when he'd be in the Bay Area. Out walks Paul McCartney, and of course everyone is shocked that there was no media leaks beforehand and the place was half empty (only holds 4,500). Did she go backstage afterwards to snarf an autograph for her Beatle-fan son? Noooooooooo! Oh well. "I told Allen I'd go to a book signing of his later in the week, so I left early, knowing I'd see him then." Christ. Anyway, she said they rocked the house and that I was in good company as one of Allen's accompanists. I wish I shared Paul's bank balance as well!

Levi: So you've jammed with Allen Ginsberg? Believe it or not, I actually find his music very pleasant. He has a voice like an operatic frog, but there's some strange lilting-ness to it that I find very contradictory and interesting. When did you play with him, and what did you play?

John: Allen was kind enough to invite me along on gigs he did during the seventies while visiting the Bay Area. I was living in Santa Cruz at the time. We only performed together a few times, but a couple shows stand out in my memory.

The first was when my rock band at the time was playing as house band at a nightclub called the Sail Inn near the Portola Avenue beach. Ginsberg somehow found us and showed up unannounced with Peter Orlovsky and others in tow. I convinced the band to take a break so I could get Allen up there to do his thing, and I joined him on electric guitar. He played his harmonium and Peter played banjo. I was used to Allen simply reading his poetry and wailing on finger cymbals, so this configuration was new to me. He told me he had learned the blues and jammed with Dylan on three-chord progressions, mostly in the key of "C." He had recently done local shows accompanied on guitar by Barry Melton of the Fish, and he now needed a new sideman as Barry was busy somewhere else. I said I'd be honored.

That first night we played about a half hour on slow, dirge-like blues chords over which he sang poems. I peered into the audience to see the club's owner and the few patrons that were left in attendance staring with their mouths agape. They hadn't a clue and we nearly lost our cushy gig there, but Allen liked it and soon called me for others. The best was a benefit for Chet Helms and the Family Dog called the Tribal Stomp held at the Greek Theater in Berkeley in '78. It was a big thrill for me because I got to meet all my hero bands from the sixties backstage. Allen even paid me; what a deal.

Levi: I'm a pretty big Beatles fan too. My favorite's are Lennon's solo albums. I like Yoko's albums quite a bit as well. McCartney is sometimes good ... he had good taste in partners.

John: I've never listened to Yoko's stuff, but if it's anything like *Two Virgins*, I'll pass. I was caught by the Beatles at the perfect age to experience the mania, and I confess that I never got over it. Paul, although more traditional in style, was a great songwriter when with John, but lost it without him. I don't think

A LITERARY GENERATION'S LEGACY

Lennon did as well on his own, either. I think as I did in the sixties: Lennon = God.

Levi: What are your siblings up to?

John: My two older sisters still live in California and we get together whenever possible.

Cathy, 47, and her husband George live near Sacramento. Their three kids are now grown and off on their own. Cathy's a health care professional and teacher who moved out of the house as a teenager and got married so I didn't hang out with her as much as I would have liked as an adult. We're very close but only see each other on rare visits a couple times a year because of the distance between our homes. She's got a lot of Neal stories of her own of which I only catch glimpses when we're able to meet. She's happy to stay more out of the mainstream Beat lore network.

Jami, 45, and her husband Randy live near Santa Cruz. They have a daughter, Becky, 14. They lived in Los Gatos up until a year ago, so I've kept in fairly close contact with Jami over the years. "How's my sweet little Jami?" Jack would write to Carolyn in the early '50s. Cathy and I weren't exactly treated like chopped liver, mind you, but Jami was such a doll and everyone's favorite. They're both in Jack's books a lot (I was the runt of the litter and too young). Jami works in a dental office, and often wonders why she and Cathy rarely get mentioned in these Neal articles (thanks for asking, Levi). Jami has shared some amazing memories of Dad with me on occasion, like the time her boyfriend's band was playing The Barn in Scotts Valley (infamous psychedelic dance hall/Prankster hangout) and Neal was so high she had to look after him all night in the black-lit, postered catacombs of the place. Someday I'll record her tales.

Curt Hansen is my half brother by Dad's short-lived marriage to Diana in New York. Although I've only met him twice in person, he's a great guy and we keep in touch. He and his wife Debbie came out for a weekend visit in '94 and we had good talks. I couldn't recall our first meeting at Carolyn's in 1969, but then again I can't recall most of that year anyway. Curt is the program manager at radio station WEBE in Connecticut.

Levi: Jack and Allen Ginsberg seemed to have felt alienated when your parents become devotees of Edgar Cayce's mystical philosophy. At the same time, Cayce's influence seems to have been a good one for Neal, and for your parent's marriage. What do you think of all this? Did they teach much of it to you? Is your mother still influenced by it, and are you? It almost seems, from what I've read, to have been your family "religion."

John: Edgar Cayce represented a great alternative to the dogmatic Catholicism in which Neal was raised, and my parents shared his philosophy with us kids at a young age. My mother insists it was not the man, but his "channeled information" that is important. Apparently he was just a farmer from Alabama or somewhere.

They didn't raise us to be ignorant of the basics, though, and sent us to Sunday school first. That's us on the way to church on

A LITERARY GENERATION'S LEGACY

Easter Sunday, 1957, on the cover of *Grace Beats Karma*. I wasn't fond of going to church, except for getting ice cream cones at Foster's Freeze next door after the ordeal. After about a year of that they announced they would keep us home Sunday mornings, but we had to listen to them for an hour as if it were school. This news was like being let out of jail when you're seven years old, and we heartily approved. They would read from different alternative books including Cayce and other metaphysical stuff, and in that context it didn't seem way out at all. Also, they weren't fanatics by then on Cayce or anything else, as described earlier by Kerouac when it was fresh.

We grew up with an understanding of karma and reincarnation that I took for granted until I went to public schools and realized this knowledge wasn't normal among my peers. In that regard it was somewhat of a cruel shock to learn that everyone didn't believe this stuff, and I had to adjust to other points of view. Still, I don't regret adopting their perspective. They thought much in organized religion was distorted, except for the basic concepts that started them, like the Golden Rule. My experience since then has resulted in similar thinking.

My mother hasn't changed her outlook much over the years, but doesn't "preach" it much anymore. She seems secure in her knowledge of how the universe works. Her basic beliefs remain unchanged, which is comforting, and they still ring true for me.

I think after Jack had embraced Buddhism so desperately he was unwilling to shift gears again when confronted with Neal's Cayce rap and tuned it out. Just a theory; I was awfully young.

66

(On November 5, the *New York Times Magazine* printed an article called "Children of the Beats." Written by Daniel Pinchbeck (son of Jack Kerouac's one-time girlfriend Joyce Johnson), it featured profiles of John, Neal's other son (by a different woman, Diana Hansen) Curt Hansen, Jan Kerouac, Parker Kaufman, Lisa Jones and others. This article caused a bit of a stir with its tragic overtones – the thesis seemed to be that all the Beat writers had been despicable parents. I wrote to John that I didn't think the article captured what I saw as the positive side of his life.)

John: I agree with you about the article's overall negative tone. Even I came off sounding like I thought the whole era was trivial. My biggest beefs were that he only mentioned the book *Heart Beat*, not *Off the Road*, as my mother's principal work. Christ, it's been out of print for twenty years, and sales of *Off The Road* could have been helped by a mention in a piece with this kind of circulation. Also, no mention of my sisters, who, last I checked, were Neal's kids as well. And what's up with this "John Allen?" I don't recall calling myself that when we talked. I suspect he was trying to allude to the Kerouac/Ginsberg namesakes, but he never mentioned them! And shouldn't one say "His mother IS Carolyn Cassady", not "WAS?" At least his spelling was correct.

I think he was out for sensationalism in the Neal stories he recorded, similar to the Beats-suck-as-parents theme in the other interviews. The only story he bothered to print was about Neal's decline, although I gave him two hours worth of upbeat, funny ones. Pat noticed he wasn't writing in his notebook during these. Possibly because when he would earlier ask things like "what did you learn from all this?" or "how were you affected?" I'd blow him off and continue with stories (similar to our interview?) and he might have felt slighted. At least you were compassionate and let me ramble.

All things considered, I'd say it's about a C+. I've had worse showings, but certainly better. The piece in the Metro (San Jose) from about '88 comes to mind as more accurate (and pages longer). Too bad it was not as widely read.

Levi: One other thought I had – since some of the other "children of the Beats" don't seem like the type to have kids, it would have been nice to mention that you have a son. Speaking of which, what does he think of all this Neal publicity? Did he like the article?

John: Yeah, that would have been nice if the portrait of him above my head [in the photo of John that accompanies the article] which article had mentioned Neal's grandson. His name's Jamie, after my sister, cruel parents that we were. I came home last night and said his picture is in the *New York Times* so he's famous. That's a chalk my mom drew in London in '92. Jamie hasn't read much Beat stuff and probably doesn't understand what the big deal is, but he thinks it's bitchin' to have a famous grandfather and to see our name in stuff all the time.

Levi: Do you talk with Jan Kerouac, Jack's daughter?

John: I think Pat early on sent you a description of when I spoke at Jan's benefit show in San Francisco earlier this year. I got loaded and lost my wallet, which Kesey found and gave to Gerry Nicosia to return to me, Jeez. I was given a pretty cool photograph taken of Jan and I sitting together while giving interviews earlier that day which I can try to send to you somehow. An historic meeting. It's too bad her life's been rough lately. Makes me not feel so bad about my own life, though. We all have demons to exorcise.

I proposed to her at our first meeting in North Beach in the early '70s. She was lookin' good back then, and I thought, "what a perfect match-up!", historically speaking, at least. What would Jack and Neal have thought? I forget what her response was, but we never married, as I recall.

Levi: What about Bill Burroughs, Jr?

John: Bill showed up at my mother's house in Los Gatos around '73. At that time her place was party central, and I recall some crazy times during that era. I had just returned from a year's travel across the US, and my sister Jami and her husband Randy were living with Carolyn. I had been home about a week, sleeping on the couch because Jami and Randy had claimed my old room in my absence, when they threw a giant party in the half-acre dirt back yard. It was a Memorial Day party, to celebrate all our gone "gone" friends.

We built a big stage at the back of the lot on a hill. There were three rock bands and Allen Ginsberg did a long set, singing, chanting, and reading poetry. He had a broken leg from slipping on the ice at his place in Cherry Valley, New York, and sat cross-legged on a rug with his cast sticking out in front and incense burning. The police were mellow about the crowds and a good time was had by all. Wait a minute, what does this have to do with Burroughs? He wasn't even there yet. I know, background color about my mom's house in those days. I soon moved to Santa Cruz, but the next spring I found they had built a huge vegetable garden in the back yard complete with grass trails through it with benches and bird baths and stuff.

There under a tree toward the back was this short, stocky guy with long hair and a scruffy beard with a gallon of red wine in his lap talking to Jami. They were half lit and laughing a lot, so naturally I joined them. Bill Jr. was only working on his first liver in those days and was quite lucid and witty. Everyone seemed to migrate to Carolyn's at one time or another. We would have wild all-night discussions in the living room. My mother recently sent me an audio tape she found of one of those nights, but I was so high that poor Bill couldn't get a word in edgewise, I was talking so much. It's an embarrassment, except for one stretch where we're all talking at once, Mom included, while completely ignoring the others. That part's funny.

Anyway, I didn't see Bill for a year or two. When he arrived at my house in Santa Cruz he looked thin and wasted. The first thing he did was lift up his shirt to show me the scar, more like a hole, left from his recent liver transplant, a new procedure at the time which he had just received in Denver. I nearly hurled, but helped myself to the jars full of Valium which he spread on the kitchen table. He was understandably tired and our subsequent discussions weren't nearly as lively as in the past. The great local writer William J. Craddock sought him out and had us over for dinner. Craddock was a big fan of Neal's and seemed to enjoy having the second generation converge at his house.

The sad day came when Bill was feeling so poorly that I insisted on driving him to the emergency room at Dominican Hospital in Santa Cruz. They immediately whisked him back to Denver and within days he was dead. Although his father's money gave him a second chance with a transplant, I think it was too little, too late. He was one of the casualties of the tragic side of these lost artist types. Daniel Pinchbeck was just twenty years too late to interview Bill Jr.

Levi: Tell me about the "Dunkels". [Ed and Galatea Dunkel were two of the more colorful characters in "On The Road." Like most of Kerouac's characters they had their real life equivalents, Al and Helen Hinkle, close friends of the Cassady family.]

John: I ran into Al Hinkle in the supermarket last night. On the way home I flashed on the fact that the suburban ladies pushing shopping carts around us had no clue that Big Ed Dunkel from *On the Road* was chatting with Dean Moriarty Jr. in the frozen food isle (nor would they have cared). He's in his late 60's and looks great; just got back from a month in Denver visiting an older sister in Neal's old neighborhood. He lost his wife Helen to cancer last year which was heavy for all of us.

A LITERARY GENERATION'S LEGACY

Levi: That blows my mind about Big Ed Dunkel ... I didn't know "Galatea" had died, either. I always enjoyed that part in the book where she chews your father out and he goes and sits on the stoop for a few minutes considering it, then, without a word, gets up and continues with his life. Sometimes you gotta just do that ...

John: Helen Hinkle was an extremely wise woman. I liked that scene, too. It's almost excruciating to read because she's so right and Dean is so foolish. Helen called it like it is. I was so grateful that I looked her up in recent years and had long talks with her about them all in the days, not knowing her time would be short. I almost missed her altogether. They've lived in the same house for over forty years, and just a few miles from my current address, but I just never got around to seeing them much until about three years ago. The Metro also did an excellent piece on the Hinkles a couple years ago. They were a big part of it all and no one knows. Helen was so funny. She liked to remind me that she used to change my diapers when I was a baby, jeez. She'd sit there and smoke cigarettes, drink coffee and curse during her stories; what a character. Al is more of a mellow talker and a bit long-winded, but has some great stuff from the Denver days.

Levi: Are you in touch with Ken Kesey and Ken Babbs?

John: I consider Kesey and Babbs friends. I saw neither of them for about 15 years, although I kept track of them. Kesey was at my first wedding in 1975, then I didn't run into him again until around 1990. I've seen them both at various functions quite a bit since then. They're being more visible as of late. I took 8mm movies of Kesey and Neal, along with Ginsberg and others, when they visited our house in Los Gatos. They were an already infamous bunch that I wanted to record for posterity. Alas, those films have been lost. I next went to visit Ken on his farm in Eugene in '72 with another 8mm camera. Those films I still have and plan to transfer them to video someday.

(During the period that John and I were conducting this interview I received an e-mail asking if I knew anything about the myth about "Cassidy's" habit of flipping a hammer and catching it, which Tom Wolfe wrote about in *The Electric Kool-Aid Acid Test*. The person wrote: "Somewhere, sometime, somebody said that Cassidy used the hammer as a practice to sharpen his perseption [sic]. Something about that it took about 1/30th of a second to perceive something happening in the world and that he used the hammer as an exercise to shorten the recognition time." I thought this seemed a bit silly, but forwarded the mail to John to see what he'd say, asking if he wanted me to keep sending him stuff like this.)

John: Sure, I like to be bothered by silly stuff. Keeps me current.

As far as this guy's search, why anyone would look for meaning in this hammer thing is beyond me, but that theory sounds vaguely familiar. First we must correct his spelling on "Cassady" and "perception". I guess you receive mail from scholars and otherwise.

73

A LITERARY GENERATION'S LEGACY

My take on the hammer is that by that stage of the game Neal was, sadly, so loaded up on crank that he simply needed something to fiddle with. He retained massive arm strength, and the hammer suited his ancient wheel karma railroad/car/tool trip. Tim Allen on steroids.

Also, he always had a penchant for juggling and sight gags a la W.C. Fields. Inept at real juggling, he would flip objects (pencils, etc.) and catch them on the same "handle" end. The game was to count how many flips he could go before missing and starting over at "1." He would frequently get into double digits, to the delight of us kids (we were easily entertained). He would also do this trick, a lot when we were young, where he'd balance on one leg, grab his ankle and leap over his other leg, nearly knocking his chin with his knee, and land upright again on one foot. He couldn't do it as well after his various railroad accidents stiffened his legs, so he'd go careening across the room on landing, YAAAA, and we'd giggle all the more.

But I guess this stuff isn't nearly as mystically legendary or mysterious as his trying to shorten his recognition time to 1/30th of a second or whatever. People can believe whatever they like if it helps get them through the night, right?

(Pat, who was on the email cc: list for much of these conversations, chimes in here)

Pat: Hey, at the least the guy has something to keep him busy. Kesey rambled on and on in *Electric Kool-Aid Acid Test* about 1/30 of a second being the least amount of time in which a human could perceive something. He said most humans took much longer with the exception of Neal Cassady, the fastest man alive. It's something along those lines. He also said that Cassady never dropped the hammer unless he wanted to make a point that something was happening and that people should pay attention to it. 'Course, Kesey was tripping his ass off quite a lot then and that's conducive to theories. I had friends who believed Jerry Garcia communicated with them at concerts by reflecting the light off his glasses into their eyes.

John: Would that we all could make mistakes and have people go "oooh, aaaah, it's cosmic!"

POETRY AT THE OLD LONGSHOREMAN'S HALL

by Don Carpenter

It was the spring of 1964 and Gary Snyder had just come back from several years in Japan, and I thought it would be a good thing for him to have a public reading of his new poems. Up until then the poetry readings I had gone to had been chaotic and profitless (for the poets), and so the trick would be to set up the reading on a professional basis.

Some years earlier I had hosted a poetry reading in my basement in Portland, Oregon, with Gary Snyder and Philip Whalen reading, and it had been awful, all except for the poetry. It was too crowded, too hot, and when we passed the hat to pay for the wine we only got $1.75. A window got broken and somebody trampled my nasturtiums. But hell. This time, I resolved, there would be planning, care lavished on every detail, the audience would be comfortable and the poets would make a few bucks.

I asked Snyder and Whalen if they would like to read together again if I did all the work and they got all the money, and they agreed. But, it turned out, Donald Allen, the redoubtable editor and translator, who sprung the Beat Generation on the world with Evergreen Review Number Two, had it in mind to offer Snyder and Lew Welch in a joint reading. A meeting was called at my apartment on Jersey Street and it was quickly agreed that we should pool forces.

Actually, it was a wonderful combination. The three poets were all friends, had gone to Reed College together, living in the same house at 2121 Lambert Street. All three were deeply involved in Zen, not Marin County Zen but the real thing (or perhaps I should say the unreal thing). But they had totally different personalities and wrote totally different poetry. Gary Snyder was quiet and scholarly, living simply, an anthropologist as much as a poet and able to read and write both Chinese and Japanese. Philip Whalen was big and soft-looking, but not soft. He loved to talk and laugh and he knew very nearly everything. He was a man of extreme courage, and refused to work at anything but being a poet. "I had a job once", he told me, "and I don't ever want to have another one." Sometimes this meant he would go days without food, but he always managed to pull through and do his work.

I didn't know Lew Welch well at the time, but I liked very much his intimate raffish and quite beautiful poetry, what little there was of it. Tall, thin, handsome, always wearing a crooked smile, Welch liked to think of himself as a hip conman. He liked to drink and sit in the Jazz Workshop and listen to good music. He loved Sausalito and the no name bar and he loved to play pool and skulk around the Tenderloin. He had just come down from the Trinity Mountains where he had been living in a little cabin for two years, writing, and, incidentally, winning a turkey in a turkey shoot. He was a complex and interesting guy, who had worked in Chicago as an advertising writer, he had traveled crosscountry with Jack Kerouac, and I don't know what all.

77

A LITERARY GENERATION'S LEGACY

I didn't start getting nervous until I looked at the hall. The Old Longshoreman's Hall on Golden Gate looked gigantic and empty. I had never seen more than a couple of hundred people at a poetry reading (the night Allen Ginsberg first read 'Kaddish') and this damned place could hold six hundred or more. But the price was right, $75.00, and so with a gulp I wrote out the check. It was all the money I hoped to lay out and nearly all I had in the bank. I expected to get it back off the top, should as many as seventy-five people show up and pay their dollar. We decided to keep the price low so that people with limited funds could come.

Publicity, that was the trick. We would make a handbill, get somebody to run off copies for free, and plaster North Beach with them. The poets would make big posters and put them up in key places like City Lights Books and Mike's Pool Hall. Up to now both the Chronicle and the Examiner had been icy to North Beach and poetry, but we would change all that, we would shower them with photographs and press releases. I would badger my friend Ralph J. Gleason and he might announce the reading at the bottom of his column, although he had never done anything with poetry before. It would be a snap.

But that looming empty cavern of a hall still kept me awake nights.

Lew found a friend who volunteered to run off our handbills, if we would only come up with a design and furnish the paper to print it on. Don Allen and the poets were busy with a scheme of their own, to print up one poem from each poet in his own calligraphy (the three had all studied under Lloyd Reynolds at

Reed), and so, biting my lip, I went down to Flax's and bought sheets of rubber letters. It was simple, all you had to do was place the little letter where you wanted it, rub it with something hard (I used the rounded end of a fountain pen) and the letter would stick, and you go on to the next letter. Simple. It took me two days, and I never worked so hard or sweated so much or cursed so hopelessly. But finally the thing was done, and we printed up 500 of them, posted them everywhere, mailed them to everyone we could think of, and finally realized we were committed to this thing. Not just a reading, but a damned successful one.

I called Gleason and told him what was up and he laughed and said he'd be delighted to help in any way. On the phone he told me how to get announcements on the radio, and that I should hand-carry the press releases and pictures to the papers. Then a few days later I drove Lew over to Berkeley to meet Ralph. It was a wonderful afternoon, full of ripe conversation and jazz, and as a result Ralph gave over an entire column to Lew and our reading, called "Bread vs. Mozart's Watch." It was about how poets usually never got paid (Mozart was often paid off with a watch) and how we were going to try to change that. "If you can pay the printer, you can pay the poet", Lew often said.

Jim Hatch the photographer was unearthed somewhere and we had a photography and wine-tasting session at Gary's tiny apartment on Green Street. I wrote up press releases, mailed them to the radio stations, hand-carried them to the newspapers and began to sweat in earnest. We were all having a lot of fun, but that didn't mean anything. Gary and I went down to Market

A LITERARY GENERATION'S LEGACY

Street and bought a huge roll of tickets for the door, ate hot dogs, and that was about all there was to do.

On the night of the reading, June 12, I came two and half hours early, to fiddle with the sound equipment and because I couldn't stand waiting around at home, and was astonished to find that some people were already there, sitting on the steps or hanging around the lobby. Crazy people, I thought, and went on in. Don Allen was there in the lobby, arranging the broadsides on a big table. He gave me a nervous smile and I went backstage, where the three poets were reacting in their own ways to stagefright, Lew jacked up and visibly nervous, Gary tense and short-tempered and Phil Whalen calm and quiet.

"People are already out there", I said.

Yes, they had noticed. Had I checked the sound equipment? I went out on the stage and turned on the equipment and positioned myself behind the microphone. A mob of poets and their friends marched into the hall and took choice seats, led by Jack Spicer.

"I can't hear you", Spicer said critically.

I turned it up. "Can you hear me now, Mister Spicer?" I boomed.

I went out front again to bask in it. I was feeling very good, not nervous at all anymore. More people were coming all the time, filling the lobby and spilling out onto the front steps. I went outside. There was Ralph Gleason, come over to cover the event. He introduced me to two record company executives, who were there to tape the reading. And mobs of people milling around. This was getting to be fun!

But in the press of other matters, I had made a near fatal mistake. I had forgotten to put somebody at the door to take money and issue tickets. I rushed back into the building. Sure enough, people were entering the hall and taking seats without having paid (of course Spicer and his friends all had complementary seats).

"Hey!" I yelled into the hall, "come back out here and pay!" Many laughed, and a few came back out sheepishly and gave me their dollar. Dollars were being shoved at me from all directions. I had to make change, tear tickets and watch the door all at the same time. Across the lobby, Don Allen was selling broadsides by the dozen, and looked as harried as I felt. At last an old friend, Rick Rubin, took pity on me and helped me out, but we had easily lost a couple of hundred dollars.

The place was packed, and the crowd had an expectant air. Something really good was going to happen that night and they were here to be part of it. Eight hundred of them, lovers of good poetry, the cream of the Bay Area.

Lew led off, and it was the perfect choice, although there had been some fear that he would read too long. He was a master at reading. He was funny, intimate, in tune with the audience (and they with him), and obviously enormously pleased by the size of the response.

A LITERARY GENERATION'S LEGACY

Whalen came next, and if the crowd had loved Lew, they adored Philip, who read some of his best and funniest stuff and left the audience exhausted.

Gary came last. His poetry is not as funny as that of the other two, but it had other equally responsive elements, and the audience sat rapt under the sound of his voice, and when he would come to the end of a poem sometimes there would be only silence or an occasional "Whew!" But at other times a poem would bring down the house.

Afterward we all rode in the same car up to Gary's apartment, where we counted the money and then hid most of it in the oven. The rest we took down to Tosca's in North Beach, where everyone was waiting to celebrate. The reading had been a great artistic success, and we were entitled to a great blowout. Which we had.

When the dust cleared and I had been paid off, the poets each had a little over a hundred dollars apiece. Nobody held it against me that I had let other hundreds escape. "Hell", said Lew, "A hundred bucks for half hour's work? Not bad!"

That was all a long time ago. Gary Snyder has gone on to win many honors, including a Pulitzer prize, and is a leading figure in the ecology movement. Lew Welch, troubled by poverty and alcoholism, went into the mountains never to be seen again. Phil Whalen has become a Zen monk.

THE ALLEN GINSBERG BEAT-L VIGIL

(What follows is an extract from the BEAT-L mailing list, an Internet forum dedicated to the discussion of Beat literature run by Bill Gargan of Brooklyn College. It covers the interval immediately after the sudden announcement of Allen Ginsberg's severe illness, which was followed the next day by the announcement of his death. A famous vigil took place at Allen Ginsberg's bedside during these last hours, as his old friends arrived to say goodbye. The BEAT-L vigil took place at the same time.

Re-reading this exchange years later, I treasure the way this long conversation captures the mood of a moment. The sometimes messy, constantly overlapping discussion threads capture the chaotic, multi-threaded nature of every Internet discussion. The sudden outpouring of spontaneous poetry and poetry quotations here seems to be very Ginsberg-ian, and very Beat.

We pick up with the first mention of Allen's terminal illness, arriving in the middle of a mild, friendly flame war (this mailing list was prone to such flame wars) discussing, of all things, whether Ginsberg's poem "America" was patriotic, unpatriotic or ambivalent. – Levi)

A LITERARY GENERATION'S LEGACY

Date: **Wed, 2 Apr 1997 16:57:36 +500**
From: **Bil Brown**
Subject: **Re: ambivalence**

> *Could Ginsberg's ambivalent attitude toward America*
> *be any more effectively conveyed than in its articulation*
> *in "Howl"? "where we hug and kiss the United States*
> *under our bedsheets, the United States that coughs all*
> *night and won't let us sleep."*
> *Cordially,*
> *Mike Skau*
> *4/2/97*

Just in from a VERY reliable source:

YOUR Mr. Ambivalence, Allen Ginsberg, has terminal cancer.
Let's be nice to him for a little while. ok.

Bil

Date: **Thu, 3 Apr 1997 12:51:52 -0800**
From: **Levi Asher**
Subject: **Poetry's Final Subject (fwd)**

Sad news confirmed ...

> *Date: Thu, 3 Apr 1997 10:59:58 -0800*
> *From: digaman@hotwired.com (Steve Silberman)*
> *Subject: Poetry's Final Subject*

Allen Ginsberg has inoperable liver cancer, and "four to twelve months" to live.

Beams to our teacher and friend.

Love,
Steve

Date: Thu, 3 Apr 1997 17:45:47 EST
From: Bill Gargan
Subject: Re: ambivalence

Allen was fond of quoting Trungpa's words on Bill Burroughs Jr. when he was ill:"He will live or he will die. Both are good." I imagine Allen is better prepared than most of us for the end. Let's hope, however, that the doctors are wrong in giving him only three months. Meanwhile, let's all give him our friendship and support in the time left for us on earth together.

Date: Fri, 4 Apr 1997 12:09:14 -0500
From: Howard Park
Subject: A Comet Dims...

Allen Ginsberg was, and is, a shining light that illuminates the world with a relentless spirit of truth and love. This man has spoken truth to evil in all its forms - the evil of totalitarianism, be it communism, capitalism, fascism and every other ism of our age.

A LITERARY GENERATION'S LEGACY

As his body fails, I'm moved to reflect on the only serious discussion I ever had with him, almost exactly a year ago. It was about hope, joy and optimism, qualities of beat writing which I believe are often overlooked. Allen never shied away from the dark side of things in his art but I have always felt that there was a bedrock of joy within him.

AG's performance of "Father Death" haunts me ... but I also remember his sly, knowing squint of a smile as he sang that poem the last time I saw him do it. I see him now, in my head, with the same expression. I guess he knows something that I don't.

Date: ***Fri, 4 Apr 1997 12:05:53 +0000***
From: ***Mongo BearWolf***
Subject: ***Ginsberg, terminal liver cancer***

Hi Folks...

The rumor we heard earlier does appear to be true. Allen Ginsberg has been diagnosed with terminal liver cancer. Check out:

http://CNN.com/SHOWBIZ/9704/04/ginsberg/index.html

This is a very sad day... I'm kicking myself for discovering AG too late in life, and know that now I will probably never get a chance to see him in person.

But his work is a gift...

Date: *Fri, 4 Apr 1997 12:30:55*
From: *Richard Wallner*
Subject: *Ginsberg's cancer...*

The New York Daily News today carried an article with basically the same information. Allen has inoperable liver cancer and less than a year to live. Allen's had an amazing life and I'm sure he is looking at death as just another experience.

I always hoped that before he died, Allen would have a chance to be our national "poet laureate". But I guess he was way too anti-establishment for that to be realistic. I only hope there is a tribute organized.

Date: *Fri, 4 Apr 1997 10:01:01 -0800*
From: *John Maynard*
Subject: *Re: Ginsberg, terminal liver cancer*

mongo.bearwolf@Dartmouth.EDU,.internet writes:
>*The rumor we heard earlier does appear to be true. Allen Ginsberg has been diagnosed with terminal liver cancer. Check out:*

http://CNN.com/SHOWBIZ/9704/04/ginsberg/index.html

CNN.COM/************SHOWBIZ????????????**************

Says a lot about something, but I'm not sure what.

A LITERARY GENERATION'S LEGACY

Date: *Fri, 4 Apr 1997 13:10:46 -600*
From: *Nick Weir-Williams*
Subject: *news*

This seems to be a new update, and a very sad one.

> *Beat poet Ginsberg's health declines*

NEW YORK, April 4 (UPI) – Beat generation poet Allen Ginsberg's health has seriously worsened.

Ginsberg's doctor says the poet suffered a stroke or other complication from his liver cancer overnight.

Before last night's setback, Ginsberg was expected to live from 4 to 12 months, but his doctor now says the prognosis will be changed. The poet plans to stay in his Lower East Side home until he dies. Ginsberg, who suffers from a long-running battle against hepatitis C and cirrhosis of the liver, has terminal liver cancer.

Date: *Fri, 4 Apr 1997 14:47:21 -0500*
From: *Tony Trigilio*
Subject: *Re: Ginsberg's cancer...*

I got an email from a friend telling me about AG's liver cancer. I suspect we are going to hear the worst kinds of remembrances from the mainstream media in the next few weeks, as those threatened by AG's politics and sexuality take charge to try to rewrite his history.

Date: ***Fri, 4 Apr 1997 15:35:14 -0600***
From: ***Matthew S Sackmann***
Subject: ***AG***

I love Allen Ginsberg, let that be writ in Heaven's unchangeable heart.

Date: ***Sat, 5 Apr 1997 02:01:44 -0500***
From: ***Antoine Maloney***
Subject: ***Re: Words for Ginzy***

Recommend that anyone who has any of Allen's recorded material listen to it – listen to his "Amazin' Grace" ... he is so alive in it.

Date: ***Sat, 5 Apr 1997 12:03:16 -0500***
From: ***Timm***
Subject: ***"Allen Ginsberg Saved My Life"***

In this poem, I recorded one evening with Allen in 1993. He really did save my life.

It's an acrostic (the correct term?). The title runs down the left margin.

A.L.L.E.N. G.I.N.S.B.E.R.G. S.A.V.E.D. M.Y. L.I.F.E.
By Bob Timm (originally published in Poetry New York)

A modern executive 40th-floor office

A LITERARY GENERATION'S LEGACY

Lit by neon fruit humming tubes
Lion buddha in grey suit and tie
Even I could not detect the vision
Never a sign of his howling past

Going along 42nd Street
I think of distant highways and
Not of the immediate streets but
Suddenly he pulls out of the path of a
Bus barreling towards my thoughtful self
Ever ready for poetic graces but not
Ready for the moment when Allen
Ginsberg saved my life

Some time later we stand in line at
A Tad's Steaks ordering meat for ritual
Very raw like he said we needed
Even I could feel the snickers and stares
Directed at the crazy old man he is

My knees crack and ache in lotus form
Yet he forgets his age and folds his legs

Like an obedient faithful dog
I sip my wonton soup and wait
For the words of an ancient
East Village superstar lonely prophet

Date: Sat, 5 Apr 1997 12:29:04 -0500
From: Jeffrey Weinberg

Subject: ***Thoughts on Allen***

Anyone who was born in the 1950s like I was realizes that Allen has been there with us the whole way - If you were lucky enough to grow up in the 1950s and 1960s, maybe you had an older brother or sister who kept a copy of Fred McDarrah's "The Beat Scene" under the bed so Mom and Dad wouldn't find it. or there was a copy of Evergreen Review #2 (The SF Beat Issue) around the house. That may have been your first look at Allen. Then Howl the trial ... Howl the Fantasy recording (on red vinyl, of course) - and wasn't that Allen at the Summer of Love taking us with Michael Bowen and the other organizers into the age of Aquarius? And remember the Democratic Convention and the trial of the Chicago Seven and Allen got up in the witness box and started to meditate and chant??? And when John Sinclair of MC-5 got busted for possession of two joints, wasn't that Allen there helping to free John through great Free Sinclair rally? And all those Antiwar demonstrations throughout the sixties and into the seventies, Allen's writing continues with all the grace that God can grant a poet and Allen circles the globe for a lifetime to teach, bring peace, to write poetry, help found JK School of Disembodied Poetics, Naropa, chant, book signings,TV programs, audio, video, etc. etc. and photography and awards and time to write introductions for so many books by others to help their books sell a few more copies and because he believed in their words: Ray Bremser (poems of Madness), Huncke (Evening Sunurned Crimson), Kerouac (visions of Cody) and on and on - Do not be saddened by the news about Allen. Take a good look at Bill Morgan's massive tomes of bibliographical research: look at all that Allen Ginsberg has

A LITERARY GENERATION'S LEGACY

written and recorded in his life. Read a biography of Allen (Barry Miles' Ginsberg or Dharma Lion) (title is correct, I think) - and take a look at all that one man has done in a short lifetime (oh, yeah - concerts with Peter O and Steven Taylor around the world). Do not be saddened now. Rejoice in that Allen gave us all so much of so many kinds of so many things - different ways to look at politics, religion, poetry, photography, music and on and on - Use the life of Allen Ginsberg as inspiration. No matter whether you work the line in Detroit or teach a college course at Harvard. We can all learn something from the enormous span of achievements of Allen Ginsberg. No computer on this planet has enough memory to hold all the names of every person whose life Allen Ginsberg has touched in a positive way.

Date: *Sat, 5 Apr 1997 13:11:40 -0500*
From: *Bill Philibin*
Subject: *AG Dead ...*

Saturday April 5 11:15 AM EST

He died at 2:39 a.m. EST surrounded by family and friends, said Morgan, his bibliographer and unofficial spokesman.

The primary cause of death was cardiopulmonary arrest with the secondary cause cancer of the liver, he said. Funeral services will be private.

Ginsberg suffered for many years from hepatitis C, which led to cirrhosis of the liver that was diagnosed in 1988. The cancer was discovered when Ginsberg, who had been suffering from severe fatigue and jaundice, underwent a recent biopsy.

In 1956, Ginsberg published "Howl and Other Poems", a book of free verse considered the preeminent poetic work of the beat movement of the 1950s.

"With all the demagoguery [today], poetry can stand out as the one beacon of sanity: a beacon of individual clarity, and lucidity in every direction – whether on the Internet or in coffee houses or university forums or classrooms."
– Allen Ginsberg

Date: *Sat, 5 Apr 1997 14:26:24 -0500*
From: *Liz Prato*
Subject: *Kaddish*

Strange now to think of you, gone …

Date: *Sat, 5 Apr 1997 16:38:53 -0500*
From: *Tony Trigilio*
Subject: *Ginsberg Has Passed Away*

I just received an email note from a friend telling me that Allen passed away early this morning. The world has lost one of its brightest.

Date: *Sat, 5 Apr 1997 14:52:36 -0800*
From: *Malcolm Lawrence*
Subject: *Kaddish*

A LITERARY GENERATION'S LEGACY

(in preparation):

Hamakom yenachem etchem betoch shih-ar availay tziyon vi-yirushalayim.

"Hashem natan, veHashem lakach, yehi shem Hashem mevorach."

Boruch dayan ha-emet.

To follow up ... Ginsberg died this morning (2:39) of liver cancer and heart failure.

sigh

We lost a titan. A very gentle titan. Still, as my high school humanities teacher said, "He had a full life." And even up until the end he was still writing poetry and seeing friends on the last day he'd be conscious. ``He was very energetic," Bill Morgan said. ``He wore himself out (Thursday) talking to friends and writing poems." He wrote about a dozen short poems on Wednesday. One of the last was titled ``On Fame and Death"; others ran the gamut from nursery rhymes to politics.

"The funeral will be private. In lieu of flowers, donations should be sent to Jewel Heart Buddhist Center in Ann Arbor, Mich."

I also noticed that he died on April 5, the same day Kurt Cobain died.

I was lucky enough to see him read here in town (only once though) at the Elliot Bay Book Company back in 94 and got him to sign my copy of "Howl" afterwards.

For all you hard-core Dylan fans, remember the scene in Renaldo & Clara where he and Dylan go to Kerouac's grave?

Seems strange that he should leave before Burroughs. Then again, I personally don't believe Burroughs or Keith Richards will ever die. I mean, if they're still alive after all they've been through already, then can't help but live to see 100.

Sorry if I'm just babbling. I just think Allen was one of the most necessary poets we've ever had, who had a giant heart and was absolutely fearless.

Eliot was right ... "April is the cruelest month."

raising my glass

Date: **Sat, 5 Apr 1997 17:42:59 -0600**
From: **John Mitchell**
Subject: **Green Automobile**

Just heard (in Biermaier's B H Books on Positively 4th St.) that Ginsberg has taken off for his ultimate ride in The Green Automobile, dispensing lovely down & up Beat fearful & fearless words in his ecstatic wake, the best heart of his generation stark naked raving beatifically mad finally stopped, as the praying for the migration of his soul begins: HOWL, in spirit & deed.

I'm with you in Rockland
in my dreams you walk dripping from a sea-journey on the highway
across America in tears to the door of my cottage in the Western night

Amen

Date: **Sat, 5 Apr 1997 19:08:23 -0500**
From: **Diane De Rooy**
Subject: **Celebration of Allen Ginsberg**

Revised celebration invitation

Friends, lovers, children, members of the Beat Generation private chat room on AOL:

Allen has died. The celebration of his life goes on.

You are invited to come and share your feelings about this, read poetry and wisdom, tell stories and jokes and live the pastpresentandfuture of Allen's life in the bg private chatroom Sunday morning, from 10am to noon EDT (7 am to 9 am PDT).

We'll do the same things we did for jack on his birthday, connecting with each other and sharing joy and sadness mixed together into that special poignant concoction that only has the name "I'm alive ..."

Shanti and shalom.

Date: *Sat, 5 Apr 1997 21:15:29 -0500*
From: *Charles Plymell*
Subject: *Re: Ginzy*

Upon hearing the news Pam and I drove up to Ginsberg's Committee on Poetry farm to feed the birds and meditate.

COMMITTEE ON POETRY
April 5, 1997

Chirp, chirp, chirp
Ginzy gone
I broadcast the seeds
bread crumbs from the compost
for little animals and birds

Chirp on the phone, chirp on the radio
broadcasting them seeds
Janine left a message on the phone
I read it in chirp cyberspace

Up Lancaster St. we drove
past the bank on East Hill Road
New house where'd you come from
another house along this road

A LITERARY GENERATION'S LEGACY

that one didn't used to be there
yet another on the way to the farm
that was the idea of a farm for poets, etc.

The great view of the Mohawk Valley
its early spring mauves and browns
old crops of gold fields stalks

Didn't take the shortcut where
Ray froze his fingers round a beer can
walking to Cherry Valley in a blizzard

Turn off the paved road
Bad hill bad ruts from spring washes
Peter needs to get that tractor
and haul some dirt and gravel

Like he usta with the manure spreader
Julius faithfully standing on the hitch
Big tractor at the corner
have to walk in here
Roads all wet, parts covered with snow

Hear the birds already
Get the bread pieces
throw a few
tie my shoe

Walk down the slushy ruts

through mud and snow
old craggily cherry tree
must be a hundred

You said the old ones were wiser
"broadcast" the bread a metaphor
when you were born, tho most had radio
more bread for the bashful birds

Stop here to rest and share
my hard bagel with the birds
hmm. that doesn't taste bad
maybe I'll eat it meself.

Hardly a sound up here in hushed forest
the snow is silent in the deer tracks
Pam says the daffodils are in bloom

I'll put some bread crumbs on the porch
not on this chair with peeling paint
Bread on the old maple tree
bread on the rock for innocent creatures

A rag is hanging on the old clothesline
and the barn door needs repair
the whole barn actually, I'll leave
some crumbs by the outhouse and
the barn and the cherry tree

On the road back a woodpecker

A LITERARY GENERATION'S LEGACY

breaks the silence, hammering perfectly
like a Whitman carpenter
Burdock sticks like Velcro
Bread on the windowsill
bread on the rock

Old truck rusting away
new tires rotted in place
never helped anyone
get anywhere or nowhere anymore.

The air always changes on East Hill
like the atmosphere of heavens
the stars come down to
a respectable level in
case you need to chat with 'em

It is heavy now and the sun is
burning like chrome in the grey sky
the woods are mauve and brown dark green
the green and grey neglected cottage
weathers by the green and grey pound

The mountains and the sky are all blue
various shades enshrouding the Evergreens
white birch arises from moss green rock
of old hills and forests

You walked me to the boundary
twenty-nine years ago

probably talking of Whitman and Death
Now you know

Date: *Sat, 5 Apr 1997 19:01:44 -0800*
From: *James Stauffer*
Subject: *Re: In Memorium*

We will all miss having Allan in our dimension, but there probably isn't much to be sad about. He lived a very fully realized 70 years. I will sit down tonight and dig out some good buds to fill the pipe and smoke to Allan and read some of the old poems. Maybe tonight he will be back with Jack and Neal and Hunke and all the others who went on before him – or spend some time comparing visions with William Blake. We will miss him.

Date: *Sat, 5 Apr 1997 20:53:33 -0600*
From: *David Rhaesa*
Subject: *ginsberg april 97*

Ginsberg
i remember the time
i thought
i was
you
in a hospital
in Saint Joseph or Rock Island
(they run together)
and if I'd been right
instead of

A LITERARY GENERATION'S LEGACY

psychotic
i'd be gone
and you'd still BE
and perhaps
everyone would be better off :)

Date: *Sat, 5 Apr 1997 23:05:21 -0800*
From: *mwbarton*
Subject: *allen has passed*

the muses will sing elegies to a poet who will live in song and
word for longer than we. allen ginsberg has passed.

Date: *Sun, 6 Apr 1997 01:01:13 EST*
From: *Dylan Nomad*

Allen Ginsberg, forever in our hearts and eyes and quiet
midnight thoughts. Goodnight in heaven.

Date: *Sun, 6 Apr 1997 00:22:51 -0600*
From: *Matthew S Sackmann*
Subject: *AG*

Friends,
I just heard that Allen Ginsberg died today? Is this true? God, I
hope not. Buddha, I hope not. SOMEONE, TELL ME THIS IS
NOT TRUE!!

I don't know what else to say. It was very weird how i found out
because i was wandering N'Awlins with some friends, checking

out the art galleries, when i saw a posting for an Opne House at the new Orleans Zen Temple. I thought hey lets see what thats all about. We went in, and got a lovely tour of the whole place. And we went in the library. I asked if they had Dharma Bums (an attempted joke). No, but they had lots of other JK books. "By the way, did you know that Allen Ginsberg died today." AHH. I thought for sure that someone on the list wouldve said something if he died. Well, i must go perform my own little tribute for Allen. Pray for him and meditate for him and read some of his poems.

Date: *Sun, 6 Apr 1997 01:21:26 -0600*
From: *jEnnifEr*
Subject: *Voices...*

Someone please say something.
Say anything.

Date: *Sat, 5 Apr 1997 23:26:48 -0800*
From: *"Timothy K. Gallaher"*
Subject: *Ginsberg Died*

I met him once. In San Francisco in 1982 or 1981 at the On Broadway, a place above the Mabuhay Gardens (a couple blocks down broadway from City Lights). He and Corso were giving a poetry reading. It was around the time of "Birdbrain". He had a band backing him. It was called the Job.

I saw Ginsberg hanging around so i went up to talk to him. I asked him about the band he was being backed by, or

103

something. I certainly wasn't rude to him, but might have acted kind of arrogant and snobbish a bit, not cause of him but the band (you can really say "THE JOB" facetiously). It had the Dead Kennedys' drummer and I am sure I didn't think much of it (not because of the drummer per se, rather that they were like serious or something). It seemed like Ginsberg would have liked to have talked more or said more, but (I don't remember well) said the thanks-a-lot-see-ya. He seemed maybedisappointed and kind of shrugged with a "what was that all about" kind of shrug. I would have liked to have talked to him about Kerouac and blah blah blah but that seemed a pretty corny thing to do.

Seeing Corso and Ginsberg was a lot of fun. Corso had like a big accordian file and would go "a-ha" and dig through it and get a poem to read.

Date: *Sun, 6 Apr 1997 08:21:23 -0400*
From: *Marie Countryman*
Subject: *to allen ginsberg, still among us*.

allen ginsberg,
i saw you in my dreams last night,
i saw you forever electrified and leaping and bowing and praying and most
of all, i felt your great generosity of spirit lay a blessing on me and
all others in this world.
again,
allen ginsberg, in my dreams,

104

i saw you walking in the supermarket with walt whitman.
allen ginsberg,
i saw you chanting ommmm in the park in the midst of the riots
in chicago,
and,
upon rising,
i look out my window
i and see you in the leaves of grass, which now are rising from
their long
winter sleep beneath the melting snow,
i take a walk, thinking of you,
allen ginsberg:
looking down,
i see you in all the cracks in the sidewalk.
looking up
you are in the sky.
you ARE the sky.
allen ginsberg,
this spring
i will plant sunflowers for your spirit.

Date: *Sun, 6 Apr 1997 08:25:46 -0400*
From: *Andrew Lampert*
Subject: *Allen Ginsberg (1926-1997)*

...I receive all, I'll die of cancer,
I enter the coffin forever,
I close my eye, I disappear...

from THE END by Ginsberg, 1960.

A LITERARY GENERATION'S LEGACY

Published in Kaddish and Other Poems, 1958-1960
City Lights, Pocket Poet Series #14. San Francisco:1961.

A visionary, a beacon, a wizard of our oz, gone because cause and death fall between clauses and effects. I saw this poet read one evening while I matriculated at Bard College (early 1970s). The sound was gentle, more beatific then beat, if the list will permit the distinction. Of course it was the wildness and visionary force of the Beat vortex that seduced me. Ginsberg and his comrades, Kerouac and the still breathing Burroughs formulated that map, you know, the one that has the five compass points: North, South, East, West, and Center. Allen was the very good witch of the Center.

Date: *Sun, 6 Apr 1997 09:11:13 -0700*
From: *j thomas bailey*
Subject: *pome for Allen Ginsberg pt. 1*

as sun sets on chilly april day
i am filled w/ deep down drag down
low down bring down
sorrow (even though i know that's not what you would want)
right now these words fly over AP news wires
and by tomorrow will fill the heads
of millions
i went into the bathroom to look for nail clippers
and ended up
an the floor crying
(where will the words come from when you die, Allen?
tell me who to look to ...)

when Jack went to Buddha's heaven
(and before him, Neal)
you recorded sorrow and vision
and observation
(later it became a poem
 later put in a book
 much later in my hands)
and i saw your pain
and confusion
men you loved
and spent countless hours w/
(all of you becoming saints)
were suddenly gone forever
now you are much older
and sick

who will write your Kaddish, Allen?
it cannot be me
i never held you in my arms

Date: *Sun, 6 Apr 1997 10:57:11 -0400*
From: *Perry Lindstrom*
Subject: *Vortex Pedigree (for AG)*

Singularity in one being behold
the most amazing gift evaporates
before the face of the moon
held in gravity's oratory the libidinal
instrument we loved in him salvaged

A LITERARY GENERATION'S LEGACY

our each episodic awareness brought
into focus generational energy with
every naked chanting the inherent good
and splendid voice emerging unshadowed
out of catastrophic idiom and mundane
drudgery kicks the unwanted school
of life's real voice spoken in yeses and
great kisses and great vernacular
orgasm absorbed in holistic wisdom
allegory riffs and Buddhist symbol things
of themselves energy uniting every street
corner kid with poesy in heart sexy pilgrim
to Earth's ends with Blake/Whitman on lips.

Evaporates and is one now with all things
creatures/journeys/us/our own alone night
pondering on images eternal of his words
beyond words

Date: ***Sun, 6 Apr 1997 11:05:57 -0400***
From: ***"Robert H. Sapp"***
Subject: ***Re: pome for Allen Ginsberg***

I finished reading all the new posts on this machine, and i
pushed the button for the next email and onto the screen
popped the words: "No more messages".

and i just stared at that until i nearly cried and thought of an
obvious interpretation. Then i thought of j thomas' question "who

will write Allen's Kaddish" and thought of everybody's posts and all the works of others and Allen's works and thought, We all will.

Holy! Holy! Holy! Holy! Holy! Holy! Holy! Holy! Holy! Holy! Holy! Holy! Holy! Holy! Holy!

Date: *Sun, 6 Apr 1997 14:03:03 -0400*
From: *Paul McDonald*
Subject: *Thoughts on Ginsberg*

Ginsberg wrote something in an essay, NEGATIVE CAPABILITY: KEROUAC'S BUDDHIST ETHIC, where he related the Four Noble Truths and the Eightfold Path, eventually leading to a place where one "... exists with no credentials and no apologies, anymore than the sun has to apologize." What a wonderful way to live!

I'd like to share something very personal. Today, April 6, marks my seven year anniversary of sobriety, that is, being drug and alcohol free. Ginsberg's poetry has carried an inner metric pulse that resonates with my soul. A pulse I was completely unaware of during the thick of my active alcoholism/addiction and has carried me this far, and probably farther if I choose, through the spirtual journey that the craving for addiction gives way to when those of us with the disease choose to live differently.

Thank you Father Ginsberg, now reunited with Jack, Neal, Louis, Naomi, Trungpa Rinpoche, Whitman, Blake, Rumi and Milarepa, for inspiring us to sing this blues.

A LITERARY GENERATION'S LEGACY

Om Namah Shivaya

Date: *Sun, 6 Apr 1997 13:49:24 -0700*
From: *Adrien Begrand*
Subject: *Death News*

Allen, I like to think of you being welcomed into the afterlife
by yr waiting mother Naomi,
Louis smiling, anxious to carry on yr existential discussions
now that you both know what's on the other side,
Mrs. Kerouac politely saying hi but still with that disapproving
look in
her eyes,
and in the distance two figures, both looking youthful again,
in front of a green auto,
no tea, no tokay this time
("who needs it here, natural eyeball kicks, dig?")
Adios, Kral Majales.

Date: *Sun, 6 Apr 1997 16:00:15 -0400*
From: *Richard Wallner*
Subject: *Ginsberg memorial*

In reading the obituaries, I don't think enough has been said
about how large a role Allen played in the rise of Beat literature.
Allen was in addition to everything else, for many years the
literary agent for both Jack Kerouac and William Burroughs.
Allen carried "On the Road" and "Naked Lunch" and "Junky"
door to door and was ceaselessly energetic in promoting his
friends careers. In fact, it was Allen whose connections first got

Kerouac published ... he showed "Town and the City" to the right people and got Jack in the door at Harcourt Brace.

Allen was a visionary and will be missed ...

Neal Cassady (1928-1968)
Jack Kerouac (1928-1969)
Allen Ginsberg (1927-1997)

sigh

Date: Sun, 6 Apr 1997 17:41:57 -0400
From: Ginny Browne
Subject: AG Gone

Meditation On The Death of Allen Ginsberg

Planets and spirits-
Bodhisattva has risen,
petals left for us

i wade, hesitant,
through the calm
after the storm.

Date: Sun, 6 Apr 1997 18:07:22 -0400
From: M. Cakebread
*Subject: Dylan dedicates "Desolation Row" to Ginsberg
in Moncton, N.B.*

A LITERARY GENERATION'S LEGACY

Last night (4/05/97) in Moncton, New Brunswick, Bob Dylan dedicated "Desolation Row" to Ginsberg.

Date: *Sun, 6 Apr 1997 20:10:09 -0400*
From: *John J Dorfner*
Subject: *Re: Dylan dedicates "Desolation Row" to Ginsberg in Moncton, N.B.*

Bob ... i knew you were cool.

Date: *Sun, 6 Apr 1997 18:09:02 -0400*
From: *"Christopher L. Jones"*
Subject: *Ginsberg Reminiscence*

I had the honor of seeing Allen speak last March, here in Amherst. Myself and two friends huddled in the freezing cold in order to get front row seats. It was truly amazing. He opened by singing Blake's "Tyger", and read a lot of poems from *Cosmopolitan Greetings*. It came as a complete shock when, towards the end of the performance, he pulled out a copy of "Howl" and began to read it. He had to stop frequently, to take a sip of water or clear his throat, but he read it with such passion, it was almost a spiritual experience. It was as if everyone else in the auditorium had dissolved, leaving only the words themselves, resounding through the air. He closed by singing "Father Death Blues", and as this small figure shuffled out of the spotlight and into the shadows at the wing of the stage, my friend and I were overcome by the feeling that his time was drawing to a close. Unfortunately, it appears that the premonition has come true. I only wish that I could have said

something meaningful to him as I stood in line to have my copy
of "Kaddish" autographed ... Something to convey the respect
and admiration I had for him. Now, it's too late. Adios, King.

Date: **Sun, 6 Apr 1997 19:53:15 -0700**
From: **James Stauffer**
Subject: **For Allen Ginsberg**

I forget the first time
I read your poems
But can't forget the first time
I heard your voice read them.

Or the first time I saw and heard
you read them.
Riverside, must have been
65,66? You, Peter and Julius in the
VW bus. Wonderful long pony tails.
My undergrad friends,
boys and girls.
Aflutter. In Heat.
Personal messages from Lawrence Lipton
in LA.

The poet as thinking kids
Rock Star. And then that voice.
Out of size with the body.
Bardic.
Oracular.

A LITERARY GENERATION'S LEGACY

Perfect fit with those lines.
Can't hear them anymore in
Any other voice.

Then seeing you last November in San Francisco
Shrunken. Professorial Jacket and
Book bag. Sitting by Anne Murphy.
(Were you comparing girlish notes on Neal?)

Explaining yourself to more strident
Political homosexuals.

> "But I'm not just
> a Gay poet. I'm Jewish.
> A Columbia Professor.
> A Hippy. A Buddhist."

"The line in howl is the length of breath."
And you're not breathing anymore

> here.

But the voice remains
with us
at least as long as we are here
on this dirt,

> breathing.

Date: ***Mon, 7 Apr 1997 02:08:36 -0400***

From: *Jerry Cimino*
Subject: *Brushes with Ginsberg*

First read "Howl" in 1976 right out of college as AG was in Kerouac's orbit and I'd recently been blown away by *Desolation Angels* and *Scattered Poems*. Six months or a year later saw on a poster around town that Allen would be reading at the University of Maryland in Baltimore, the school I had just graduated from a few months before.

Went with a great friend Ronn Nuger, who took along his newly purchased copy of *Howl* for Allen to sign. Ronn had recently had a "vision" in his bed one night after reading Kerouac's *Visions of Gerard* that Gerard had told him his own father, who had been killed in a plane crash a year or two before, was "safe in heaven". As Ronn and I stood in line after the reading, not really understanding the significance of the chanting and the finger cymbals but still loving the poetry, it was our turn to stand in the great man's presence as he signed the book. As he was signing I asked excited and gushing, "Allen do you think Jack was a prophet?" and Allen's immediate response was, "No more than any man who speaks the truth".

Five years later I'm successful in Corporate America selling computers for IBM but still writing like a maniac nights and weekends. It's 1982 and I buy one of the earliest IBM PC's that's come out and find myself pounding on a keyboard all hours of the day and night and it's a delight for me, a purging, a true spontaneous flow "first thought best thought" laying my life out on 5 1/4 inch floppies.

A LITERARY GENERATION'S LEGACY

I feel a frustration. I'm writing a ton, all enjoyable introspective revealing self searching stuff but I feel I ought to be putting something out to the world. I ought to be trying to get published in some fashion. On a lark I mail a stack of old poems to Allen's office asking for advice along with a letter describing my dilemma and thanking him for being the one "who carried the torch" for so long. To my amazement I get back a postcard a few weeks later thanking me for recognizing his role in the movement.

Fast forward to 1992 and my wife and I have moved to California and built a bookstore. We start holding Beat events that gather big crowds. A letter to Allen's office at Naropa asking for help in tracking down a 16MM copy of *Pull My Daisy* for an event to correspond with Kerouac's birthday. A week later Allen calls the bookstore and neither my wife nor I are there... the employees are flabbergasted ... "Allen Ginsberg called here?" A few nights later my wife picks up the phone and walks into my study... "Allen Ginsberg's on the phone ..." "Get outta here ... somebody's pulling a goof ..." "No I really think it's him. He's got the information you were asking about".

Allen was cordial, businesslike, no nonsense. Says he can't commit to a booksigning but to try to schedule it thru his office in NY. Wishes us well with the Kerouac event and then "he thanks me" for spreading the message.

We're plugged in now. Carolyn Cassady comes for book signings. Ferlinghetti sends notes our way and we plop them in the store window. We're selling books nationwide with our catalog sales. I wear my 1-800-KER-OUAC button to various Beat events around the country and get my picture taken with the luminaries.

In NY at the 1994 Beat Conference at NYU I see a side to Ginsberg that was telling and funny. I'm in the Men's Room during a break between sessions. I'm washing my hands when in walks Allen followed by about a half dozen young men. Everybody's firing questions ... "Allen, what would Neal have thought of this ..." "Allen, why was it that ..." Allen very patiently and gently answered each question as it was asked, not missing a beat as he closed the door to the stall, took care of business in a manly sort of way and then finished up by washing and drying his hands. I walked out with the group amazed at what I had just witnessed ... here's a guy who still teaching as he's going to the bathroom, not fazed at all by a crowd following him and interacting with him during one of those most personal of moments! I gained a renewed respect for Allen Ginsberg that day!

Saw Allen for the last time in October with my wife at the San Francisco deYoung Museum when he did a performance with Steven Taylor for the traveling Whitney show 'Beat and the New America'. He looked frail of course, but there was a fire in his eyes and the ever present passion was in evidence.

There was trouble with the sound system and Allen was in command, irked that things weren't working perfectly but making the most of it and giving ideas from the stage as to what ought to be done to fix it. As a closer Allen led the entire audience in a group sing of "Nurse's Song" from William Blake's "Songs of Innocence", the words of which can be found at Literary Kicks ... the chorus is "And all the hills echoed" which we all pronounced from Allen's lead as "echo-ed":

And all the hills echoed
And all the hills echoed
And all the hills echoed
And all the hills echoed

This went on for minutes and minutes at the very end of the performance. It was joyful! It was gleeful! It was childlike and sorrowful and mournful all at the same time. It was Allen Ginsberg at his impactful best. We sang that chorus in the car the entire way home.

Date: Mon, 7 Apr 1997 15:48:23 -0400
From: Paul McDonald
Subject: FOR FATHER GINSBERG

Gray windy April
Ginsberg's Mahasamahdi
Now we can pray to you
And know you'll hear us
Working class Bodhisattva
Invoke yr aural shakti
And every sentient being
Pulls back the veil

Crouching in front of Muktananda's Portrait
Oakland Ashram
Chanting for a full week
In Dallas Hotel
Guru Om
On each breath

Breathe syllables
Prague '68
Kral Marales
Twenty year reign

Breathe syllables
Chicago '68
Violence does not touch you

Breathe syllables
NYC '74 mugging
Robbed of $70
Sell poem to Times
For $500

Does death really exist, Allen?

Now in the bardo
Trungpa Rimproche guiding you
Past wrathful dieties
Hungry ghosts
To be with
Jack

A LITERARY GENERATION'S LEGACY

Neal
Louis
Naomi
Whitman
Blake
Rumi
Kabir
Milarepa
Where not even dead communists/FBI
Can fuck with you now

Date: *Mon, 7 Apr 1997 15:51:33 -0400*
From: *Attila Gyenis*
Subject: *Ginsberg's Howl*

I'm sure everybody has their own Ginsberg story, this is mine. I have seen him at almost 10 events over the past five years. I have always reacted the same way at his readings - he always has a few poems that I really don't like, but just when I'm ready to despair, he comes up with the whammo killer poem that puts everything back into perspective as to why he is the poet that he is. Last year it was the Skeleton poem that was recently released on CD (it would have been nice if it had a version on it without the music), when he read it it was a steam roller that just picked up speed all on the downhill. The year before that it was the poem about food that people like to eat, ending with something about 'go ahead and eat feed your cholesterol coated arteries with rich chocolate german cake'. And then when he would talk about man's relationship with nature and the role of balance, again it illuminated the fact that he had a compassionate understanding of mankind.

But my favorite Ginsberg story is about the time he was on this panel talking about the Beats, and as some of the other presenters were giving their speech some members in the audience were complaining that they couldn't hear the speaker. Ginsberg proceeds to publicly admonish the speaker for not speaking clearly enough and loud enough, and explaining how it is the speaker's responsibility to ensure that they are projecting enough to have the audience understand them. Later, when it was Ginsberg's turn to talk, again some audience members complained that they couldn't hear. Ginsberg quickly turned to the moderator and exclaimed "Can't somebody fix these microphones!" So much for projecting.

Last year in DC at a conference at the National Portrait Gallery (in conjunction with the Rebel Writers and Painters exhibition), Ginsberg did readings and talked about the afterlife saying that he didn't believe in an afterlife. He said he could only believe in things that he can experience but he hasn't experienced death or afterlife. I wonder what he's writing about now?

Date: **Mon, 7 Apr 1997 13:42:52 -0700**
From: **mwbarton**
Subject: **coffee?**

sitting in the east village feeling a touch beat. anyone interested in having a cup of coffee and a smoke?

SLICED BARDO: FOR WILLIAM S. BURROUGHS

by Lee Ranaldo, Robert Creeley, Carolyn Cassady and Patricia Elliot

Assembled by Levi Asher

It took me a while to figure out how to memorialize William S. Burroughs, after his death on August 3, 1997.

There's something about Burroughs that makes words seem ridiculous, especially trite sentimental words about death. This is the writer, after all, who'd coined the phrase "Language is a virus". When Burroughs' fellow Beat writer Allen Ginsberg died a few months earlier, the emotional response flowed easily, as Ginsberg's own literary style was warm and highly personal. With Burroughs it would be trickier.

I had gathered a few pieces that I wanted to work with. The first was the transcript of a telephone interview conducted by poet and Sonic Youth guitarist Lee Ranaldo, which Lee had sent me along with three surprisingly great photos he'd taken when visiting Burroughs at his home in Kansas. The second two were short tributes I solicited from two writers who'd known Burroughs personally, Robert Creeley and Carolyn Cassady – not because the pairing of these two people had any special significance in the life of Burroughs, but mainly because I happened to know both their e-mail addresses. Carolyn Cassady's reply was extremely curt and not very complimentary to Burroughs, but I considered her point of view as valid as any other, and it did not seem unfitting that there should be some divisiveness within a memorial to this highly controversial personality.

The fourth piece is, I think, the most remarkable: a personal account of the Tibetan/Egyptian-inspired after-death ceremony, a bardo, conducted by Burroughs' closest friends and partners shortly after his death. This was written by Patricia Elliott, who'd been Burroughs' close friend, and who originally posted it to the BEAT-L Internet mailing list.

Unsure how to make these pieces fit together, I finally decided to follow Burroughs' own example and give up on trying to reconcile the individual parts. Burroughs had found meaning in the "cut-up" style of writing, in which sentences and paragraphs from various sources are spliced together intuitively but not logically, often revealing hidden meanings within. Getting into the spirit, I took inspiration from his title *Naked Lunch* and Ginsberg's related title *Reality Sandwiches* and decided to call this whole project "Sliced Bardo". That's it, and here it is.

As James Grauerholz says in the final section, facing the fire: Let's burn it.

ONE: LEE RANALDO'S INTERVIEW

In April 1997 I had the chance to connect via telephone with William Burroughs to ask him some questions about Morocco and the years he spent in Tanger. Having traveled there a few times myself recently, I was curious about the Maroc of the forties and fifties, when Tanger was classified an "International

123

Zone" and the laws were famously lax. We spoke for about half an hour that afternoon; I got the impression William wasn't really up for much more than that; he was alert but sounding a bit weary.

It wasn't until some months later in a Kaatskill Mountain cabin that I dug out the cassette tape to transcribe. I spent the better part of that afternoon trying to decipher his gravelly drawl, and pondering his life's journey. On two occasions Sonic Youth had the opportunity to visit him at his home in Lawrence, Kansas, where he took great pleasure in showing us jewel-encrusted knives, gun catalogues, his beloved cats, and the Orgone box out back which he'd built himself, between the pond and garden. Two days later on August 2 I heard of his death. I felt I had just been conversing with him. Barely three months separated his death from that of his lifelong friend Allen Ginsberg.

This man, who spoke of language as a virus, had become subliminal, a skewed organism, rooting under the cultural skin of our time. Imagine a world un-cut-up, without his bone-dry timing, without *The Soft Machine* or Dr. Benway. Imagine how much vital, challenging work from the last few decades, in so many fields, might not exist without him.

Later in the month, when the *New Yorker* published his final journal entries, it was clear that he could see the end coming. And what was he left with? Here is his final entry, day before he died: "Love? What is it? Most natural painkiller. What there is. LOVE." Those are the thoughts he leapt off with. Even before the words make sense, that voice is digging in. Listen to him

speak yr mind, find rock power writ in his pages, let yr fingernails
be left uncleaned.
LR 10/97

> *(loud dial tone and faint "hello, hello?"*
> *silence*
> *touch tone phone tones*
> *ringing 5 or 6 times)*

William: eh, Hello?

Lee: Is this William?

William: Yeah.

Lee: Hi William, this is Lee Ranaldo in New York City.

William: Yeah.

Lee: How are ya?

William: Oh, okay.

Lee: Well you sound pretty good.

> (static)

Lee: Okay, I wanted to talk to you, for just a few minutes this
afternoon, about Morocco, if you would.

A LITERARY GENERATION'S LEGACY

William: Just a moment, I gotta get my drink.

Lee: Okay.

   (*25 sec silence*)

William: OK.

Lee: Okay, first off, William, I'd like to say that I was very sad to hear about Allen, I know you guys have been friends for the longest time.

William: Yes. Yes, well he knew, he knew it. He faced it.

Lee: It seems like he faced it in a very dignified way, actually.

William: Yep, he told me, "I thought I'd be terrified but I'm not at all".

Lee: He did?

William: Yes, "I'm exhilarated!" he said.

Lee: Well, I suppose if anyone had the right, uh, frame about them to go out that way, it was probably him. I was hoping to get one more visit in with him before he passed on, but that was not meant to be. I'm sure a lot of people felt the same. When was the last time you saw him?

William: Los Angeles. At my show there.

Lee: I wanted to talk to you about Morocco a little bit. I've recently been to the country, a few times, and done some exploring, and I know you spent quite a bit of time in Tanger. I just wanted to pick yr brain about that a little bit. You went to Tanger for the first time in 1953, 1954?

William: Nineteen-fifty-four, I believe.

Lee: How did you end up in Morocco? What was it about the place that drew you there? I mean, today there are a lot of different romantic associations with the coast of North Africa.

William: There were a lot more then than there are now, I can tell you that. You'll notice more subdivisions now, as it's modernized and is no longer cheap. For one thing, it was very cheap then. Yeah, man, I lived like a king for $200 a month.

Lee: Did it have the same sort of appeal, then, that Berlin had in the sixties and seventies, an international zone of sorts?

William: Pretty much so. It was an anything goes place, and that's another plus.

Lee: And that was pretty available knowledge, when you went there?

William: Oh sure.

A LITERARY GENERATION'S LEGACY

Lee: Had you known Paul Bowles, or known about him, before you went there?

William: I'd read his books. I didn't know him.

Lee: Did you meet him fairly quickly after you were there?

William: Mmm, I'd been there for some time, I'd met him very slightly. Later we became quite good friends, but that was some years afterwards.

Lee: Do you enjoy his writing?

William: Very much, very much. Very particular style, particularly in the end of *Let It Come Down*, that's terrific, terrific, and *The Sheltering Sky* is almost a perfect novel. The end of that, oh man, that quote: *"At the end of the Arab quarter the car stopped; it was the end of the line."* great!

Lee: Did you know Jane (Bowles)?

William: Oh yes, quite well.

Lee: What'd you think of her?

William: Oh she was incredible.

Lee: I've heard incredible things about her, she lived quite an interesting life herself, although I guess in general women in

Morocco were very much invisible, in a certain way. Native women, at least.

William: It's a very complicated situation, very complex, and I don't pretend to know much about it. Jane Bowles was sort of known for her strange behavior. In New York they invited her to some party where all these powerful ladies were, and they asked her, "Mrs. Bowles, what do you think of all this?", and she said "Oh" and fell to the floor in quite a genuine faint. That was her answer!

Lee: Did you pretty much exist within an expatriate community there, or did you have a lot of contact with the local people? Was is easy to have contact?

William: The local people, umm, I don't speak a fuckin' word of Arabic, but I speak a little Spanish, y'know, they all spoke Spanish in the Northern Zone. My relations were mostly with the Spanish. Spanish boys. And, of course, otherwise in the expatriate side.

Lee: Right, but you didn't frequent the Barbara Hutton crowd?

William: Nooo.

Lee: There was a description, in Barry Miles book (*El Hombre Invisible*), where he said that you felt very lonely and cut off, being isolated in this corner of North Africa.

A LITERARY GENERATION'S LEGACY

William: It wasn't being in a corner of North Africa that made it so, it was the fact that I hadn't made many friends there.

Lee: Was that a strange time for you? Living there without really knowing anyone?

William: Not particularly, I've visited many places alone, many times.

Lee: Do you think that the general tenor of life in Morocco influenced the way you were writing at that point? The daily life coming out in some of the routines?

William: Probably. The more I was in that surrounding the more I liked it. More and more. Yeah, it was cheap, and then, I met this guy Dave Ulmer (?), who was Barnaby Bliss (his nom de plume). He was at work writing society columns for the Tanger paper, an English (language) paper, the *Morocco Courier*, run by an old expatriate named Byrd, William Byrd, an old Paris expat. [Ulmer/Bliss, a character of some unsavory repute, supposedly introduced WSB to Tanger's young boy homo-sex scene, and also, more importantly, to Paul Bowles]

Lee: Did you do much traveling around Morocco while you were there, or did you pretty much just stick in Tanger?

William: I'm ashamed to say, not much. I went to Fes, I went to Marrakech, and passed through Casablanca, some other places there, I forget the names of the coastal towns, and I've been to Jajouka!

Lee: Yeah, I wanted to talk to you about that, I'm friendly with Bachir Attar, and the last time we were there I went to Jajouka as well. I saw your inscriptions in his big scrapbook, and heard some stories.

William: Yeah.

Lee: How did you end up there?

William: Through Brion Gysin, more or less.

Lee: What did you make of the music?

William: Great, great. I loved it. Magic, it really has a magical quality that you can't find anymore, anywhere. It's dying out everywhere, that quality.

Lee: It still seems to be in evidence when they play today, I don't know if you've heard them recently.

William: Not recently, but I've heard the recordings, some of the recordings. Ornette Coleman made some, you know. I was there when he made those.

Lee: Excuse me?

William: I was there.

A LITERARY GENERATION'S LEGACY

Lee: You were there when he made those (*Dancing in Your Head*) recordings?

William: That's right.

Lee: Oh, gee, wasn't that in the 70's? I didn't know you were there when those recordings were happening.

William: Yeah, it was, '72, I think.

Lee: Are you still in touch with Bachir?

William: No, not really.

Lee: You were in touch with his father, I suppose.

William: Yes, I knew the old man, sure, I remember him. He was the leader of the group back then.

Lee: How many musicians would you say were in the group back then?

William: Oh, I don't know, it would vary, I'd say about 12, 15.

Lee: That's about how many there are today as well. What about at the 1001 Nights (*Gysin's restaurant in Tanger*), were the Jajouka musicians playing in there?

William: Well, various musicians. They had dancing boys in there, too. But I didn't know Brion too well, I was only there a couple of times. I didn't know him then. I became friendly with him in Paris, later.

Lee: Were you involved much with the music there, in Morocco, in Tanger? Did it make any strong impression on you?

William: Well, I like the Moroccan music very much, the music is omnipresent. I'd be sitting at my desk and hear it outside. It was all around you.

Lee: I'd like to hear your impressions of the kif smoking there, and the majoun.

William: Sure. Well, the kif smoking was, y'know, anywhere and everywhere. There were no laws.

Lee: They sort of smoke it the way people have a drink here, as a social relaxant?

William: Well, not exactly the same way. In the first place, it's pretty much confined to men, though I suppose the women get to smoke on their own. But anyway, of course majoun is just a candy made from kif, the kif, you see, is mixed with tobacco.

Lee: Right.

William: I can't smoke it.

Lee: Nope.

William: So I'd always get those boys with the tobacco, I'd tell 'em: 'I don't want the tobacco in it.' So I rolled my own, and made my own majoun. It's just a candy, it's pretty much like a Christmas pudding, any sort of candy works good, fudge or whatever.

Lee: And how did you find it? Was the high pretty pleasing?

William: Very very very much. It was stronger than pot.

Lee: Were you smoking a lot of that, or taking a lot of that, when you were writing some of the routines?

William: Yeah, sure. It helped me a lot.

Lee: The place where you spent a lot of your time there (in Tanger), the Muniria (the famed "Villa Delirium")?

William: The Hotel Muniria, yes.

Lee: Was it a hotel or a boarding house?

William: It was a hotel.

Lee: That's where you wrote a lot of the routines that became *Naked Lunch*?

William: Quite a few of them, yes.

134

Lee: And is that where Kerouac, Ginsberg and Orlovsky, those guys, came to visit you?

William: I was living there at that time, yes. They didn't, there wasn't a place in the Muniria, but they found various cheap places around very near there.

Lee: I heard Kerouac had nightmares from typing up your stuff at that time.

William: (pauses) Well, he said.

Lee: Was he the first one to actually sit down and type a bunch of that stuff up?

William: No, he was by no means the first. Alan Ansen did a lot of typing, and of course Allen Ginsberg. I don't know who was first but it wasn't Jack.

Lee: Those guys came and went pretty quickly, compared with the amount of time you spent in Morocco, I guess they weren't as enamored of the place.

William: Well they were settled somewhere else. Now for example, Jack didn't like any place outside of America, he hated Tanger.

Lee: I wonder why?

A LITERARY GENERATION'S LEGACY

William: He hated Paris because they couldn't understand his French.

Lee: His French was a Canadian dialect.

William: Those French Canadians got themselves into a language ghetto. Even the French people don't speak their language! Anyway, he'd been to Mexico quite a lot, more than many other places. He liked it there fairly well.

Lee: But he didn't like it very much in Tanger?

William: No no, not at all.

Lee: Was Tanger a violent place then?

William: It was never a violent place that I know of, never! Good God, I walked around in Tanger at all hours of the day and night, never any trouble. There's this idea that you go into the native quarter you immediately get stabbed *(laughs)* it's nonsense!

Lee: Well, people do bring back those stories now and again.

William: Well, occasionally it happens, but it is much less dangerous than certain areas of New York, my God!

Lee: If you can navigate the streets of New York you're in pretty good stead just about anywhere, I guess.

William: Yeah, that's right, you're much safer in Tanger than in New York.

Lee: Were there many travelers or tourists in Morocco at that time?

William: Not many at all. It was nice. In the summer of course you had sometimes quite a few Scandinavians, Germans *(laughs)*. Brian Howard said about the Swedes, I think it was: 'You're all ugly, you're all queer, and none of you have any money!'

Lee: There was another quote in Miles' book, you saying that you'd "never seen so many people in one place without any money or the prospect of any money".

William: You certainly could live cheaply there, yes.

Lee: Did Americans have to register with the police to live there?

William: Of course not, nothing, they had to do nothing. Well, they put in various regulations in town, you had to get a card. By the time we got our goddamn cards and stood in line and had to take all that crap, I had to get one of those in France, too, well, anyway, by that time they had another idea *(laughs)*, so your card that you had acquired was worthless.

A LITERARY GENERATION'S LEGACY

Lee: When was the last time you were back in Morocco?

William: When in the hell was it? I went there with, the last time I went with Jeremy Thomas and David Cronenberg, apropos of possibly getting some shots, y'know.

Lee: Oh, for the movie (*Naked Lunch*)?

William: Yeah, for the sets. Well, we just were there a couple of days. It had changed, not incredibly but considerably. There's been a lot of building up, a lot of sort of sub-divisions, it's gotten more westernized. There used to be a lot of good restaurants there, now there's only one, and that's in the Hotel Minza. These people I was with were saying 'Oh show me to a little place in the native quarter where the food is good.' and I said: 'There aren't no such places! Right here in your best food in Morocco, or in Tanger anyway, right in the Hotel Minza!' Well, they went out and they ate in an awful, greasy Spanish restaurant. After that they believed me!

Lee: *(laughs)* They had to find out the hard way.

Lee: Okay William, I think that that's gonna be good, that about covers the subjects I'd wanted to get at you with, on there.

William: Well fine.

Lee: I appreciate your talking to me, it's a great pleasure to talk to you.

William: Well, it's my pleasure too.

Lee: Okay, I hope to get another chance to come out and say hello to you out there in Lawrence.

William: That'd be fine.

Lee: Y'know, I have one last question for you, is that, uh, typewriter still growing out in your garden?

William: *(puzzled)* What typewriter?

Lee: Last time we were out there to visit, you had a typewriter growing in your garden amongst all the plants and things.

William: Oh, just one I threw away I guess.

Lee: Yeah, it was a very beautiful image there, with the weeds coming up through the keys.

William: *(laughs)* I guess so, I don't remember the typewriter, I've gone through so many typewriters, wear 'em out and throw 'em away.

Lee: Do you generally write with a computer these days?

William: I have no idea how to do it. No, I don't.

A LITERARY GENERATION'S LEGACY

Lee: Typewriter or longhand?

William: Typewriter or longhand, yes. These modern inventions! James [Grauerholz] has one, but I just don't.

Lee: Okay, well listen William, I thank you very much. Please tell both Jim and James thanks for their help as well.

William: I certainly will.

Lee: Okay, you take care.

William: You too.

Lee: Bye bye.

William: Bye bye.

TWO: ROBERT CREELEY REMEMBERS BILL BURROUGHS

(A few days after William S. Burroughs died, I sent poet Robert Creeley an email asking if he had any memories of Burroughs to share. He sent this back the next day. – Levi)

Here's a brief sense of what I quickly remember apropos Bill Burroughs. I can't now recall just who had told me – like peripheral gossip – but sometime in the early '50s I heard of someone who'd written a 1000 plus page manuscript with the only objective action being a neon sign going off/on over a store one could see (in the novel) across the street, etc, and of someone else who had killed his wife accidentally, attempting to shoot a glass off her head with gun he said later characteristically undershot. That was Kerouac and Bill Burroughs respectively, though for a time I reversed them not yet knowing either. In SF in the mid-fifties, and meeting (though he said we'd met briefly in '49) Allen, he gave me the Yage ms to read, which fascinated me – and you'll know I printed "from Naked Lunch, Book III" in the *Black Mountain Review* No. 7 (last issue with Allen a contributing editor and stuff from Jack, Edward Marshall's great poem "Leave the Word Alone", Cubby Selby, Phil Whalen, Gary Snyder, Mike McClure, Joel Oppenheimer, WC Williams, Ed Dorn, Edward Dahlberg, Zukofsky, Denise Levertov – etc.) I was also fellow contributor for the Big Table business – and I remember writing a statement in support when *Naked Lunch* was to be published by Grove.

We didn't meet, however, until some years later, must have been at least the mid-sixties, when he was living in London and I was there for something or other, and John and Bettina Calder had a party variously honoring various writers, particularly Burroughs. We were both John's "authors" at that point and I was staying with the Calders. Alex Trocchi was a good friend and he too was much involved. Anyhow I remember making the classic gauche comment when we're introduced, saying I was stunned with the pleasure of being able to say how much I respected his work etc etc, and then stumbling on to ask whether or not he was thinking to stay in London, etc etc – to all of which he replied briefly, dryly, yes, no – etc. In confusion I grabbed Ed Dorn who was there, and pulled him over to introduce him. Instantly Burroughs brightened, asking Ed about

A LITERARY GENERATION'S LEGACY

a recent piece of Ed's in the Paris Review – and how he'd managed the montage, etc. In short, this was work and had substance – not just banal social blather.

Thankfully I saw him again quite frequently over the years, and got past my school boy admiration (though never entirely). Anyhow we'd meet most frequently on the road and I liked his droll humor and clarity, always. One time after a talk at Naropa wherein he had recounted his experiences with a device he'd assembled permitting one to track by thought "traces" or manifests of the physical entity itself (he said he'd found one of his cats who'd got lost), he was bemused that none of the young had asked afterwards how to actually make the device, despite he had emphasized that all the necessary components could be got at any place like Radio Shack. Where's their curiosity, was the question. Another time, when mutual friends were sitting around him in sad depression over fact of an impending death much affecting him, as I came in, I am convinced he looked up and winked at me – certainly a communication, like they say.

I've always thought of him as a literalist, as I think I was – saying what he felt, understood, recognized, respected, abhorred, in very literal terms, including the fantasies. Thinking of an early common interest in Korzybski, the non-Aristotelian sense of "meaning" and syntax, his use of cut-up was very practical and effective. It broke the classic "order" or narrative as simply a "cause and effect", "historically" ordered sequence. I'd already connected with Celine, for example, and Burroughs was the solid next step.

I'd get occasional Xmas cards I am sure James Grauerholz helped get in the mail – I am grateful Bill Burroughs knew I cared, like they say. He was the impeccable "lone telegraph operator", as he put it. He got a lot done for us all.

THREE: CAROLYN'S RESPONSE

(Carolyn Cassady was another person I wrote to asking for memories of Burroughs. I wasn't aware that she felt this way about him, but I appreciated her truthful response, refusing to be sentimental in the days after Burroughs' death. – Levi)

Trouble is, I don't feel like any "tribute" to BB. As I wrote, he didn't want to know me nor I him. He represented all that I think negative and counter-productive, if not downright destructive in human life and the antithesis of what I believe we should all be about. I felt somewhat better about him when the TV interviewer asked him if there was anything in his life he regretted. Bill's reply was "Are you kidding? Everything!" I wanted to say, well, duh – I coulda told you so. "Wise men learn from the experience of others; fools from their own". I know, there's this theory that in order to appreciate the heights, you have to know the depths, but I don't agree. I have much to learn, but I don't think his way would be rewarding. So, sorry, Levi ...

FOUR: BARDO IN KANSAS

(Patricia Elliott, a friend of William S. Burroughs in Lawrence, Kansas, posted many heartfelt accounts of his last days and the *days that followed his death to the BEAT-L, an Internet mailing list where she is often a lively part of the conversation.*

I was tempted to include all of Patricia's posts here, but decided instead that this description of a Tibetan/Egyptian-inspired death ceremony had special power and was best left to stand alone. Burroughs was a writer who thrived on contradiction, and so I particularly liked the idea of a Buddhist death ceremony for a man whose strong skepticism and libertarianism did not make him a natural Buddhist in life. (Example: In a letter to Jack Kerouac, who was deeply involved with Eastern philosophy for most of his later life, Burroughs once wrote: "A man who uses Buddhism or any other instrument to remove love from his being in order to avoid, has committed, in my mind, a sacrilege comparable to castration.")

The energy and humor of clashing ideas has always been at the heart of Burroughs' art. In that spirit, here's a scene from the final act of his life story. – Levi)

All week long I didn't want to go. I felt swept with anxiety and decided about 7 times I wouldn't go. James Grauerholz, who never calls me, called me around 1 PM and said he was just checking in to make sure I knew to come. Bob, John Myers, Lena and I drove out to Wayne Propst's farm for the bardo around six. Wayne was a close and dear friend to William and an old and dear friend to me. Wayne is a mad scientist, ingenious with all things mechanical. I made a pasta salad and John Myers took a six pack.

Wayne and his family live on lush riverfront land, lots of outbuildings, scene of hundreds of experiments and gatherings. William really never missed Wayne's parties. Lena heard at school from a friend, who was also going to the bardo, that Wayne might blow something up. The excitement builds when Wayne is involved. Wayne has an old farm house, many outbuildings, trees, giant warm barn. His property runs along the Kansas River (we call it the Kaw River). Beautiful kaw valley bottoms.

The bardo is staged to be in front of the barn, in a small pasture. The big barn doors open to the pasture, flooding light from one space into another. In the middle of the pasture there was a massive dome-shaped heavy wire cage with a wire doorway. Inside were lumber, fireworks, pictures, and pages and pages of things that people brought and were bringing. I guess there were a hundred and fifty people. I knew a hundred of them, wide varieties of different folks, overwhelming for me. Actually exchanged cards with some kid that does a Burrough's site. Perfect weather, light breeze, around 60 degrees.

Around dusk, standing in front of the barn, Wayne spoke (on a nice speaker system), then introduced James Grauerholz. Now it is getting dark. James reads a farewell to William's soul letter from David Ohle, first by lighter – of course at one point you heard a little sound from James, when it got hot, and then someone brought up a kerosene lantern from the barn, and James then read a note from Giorno. Then James said a few things and explained some of the Egyptian and Tibetan

A LITERARY GENERATION'S LEGACY

Buddhistic relationships in the ceremony, tying in the significance of William's writings in his book *The Western Lands*.

Wayne goes to the dome and lights the fire. It was glorious, it grew, it swirled, popped, pulsed, danced. The cage was a dome about 12 feet high and 20 feet across. Things like pictures, posters, objects d'art, and many many papers were laid on the lumber, but things and paper also hung suspended from the cage. Once the fire flowered came Williams voice, reading from *Western Lands*. It was perfect, I swear the fire danced with his voice. The Cheshire cat had his smile but William's voice was the most evocative voice. I got up and went nearer the fire, strode around the fire, circled it three times. Most people sat in chairs and on benches in a large semi circle, music, flames, love. I stood up with James and Bill Hatke, the sparks flew wild. In the crowd was William's dentist, Charley Kincaid, (he had been one of the pallbearers at the Liberty Hall service), and he is the wildest, funniest man, with a wonderful good soul. That guy can distract you from a root canal with his wit. Fred Aldridge sat in one chair, He shot with William weekly for ten years or more. Fred is a tall skinny redhead. I've known him for 30 years. I introduced William to Fred. William was like a father to Fred's soul. Fred is a talented musician and artist, driven always to some elegant perfection. There were the New York suits standing in the barn. They seemed to be having a remarkably good time, the most relaxed I had ever seen the suits. In the crowd are such a variety of people that I am stunned but recognize that these were all people that William had built a relationship with over the 16 years he had made Lawrence his home. William loved persons rather than people, and he loved fun. It was a fun and a sober sight to see the embers chasing to the sky and think that's William's soul flying to the western lands.

I feel when William first died, his spirit was there in the room with his body. It was comforting. Then I felt his spirit whirling around the world, I almost know he went to Tangiers for a moment. I feel he is gone. We have lots to do now.

Two additional notes: Sue Brossau (David Ohles' wife) mentioned that the fire cage was one that Wayne and William had made for a bardo they'd held for Allen Ginsberg.

For a little illumination, here is, approximately, James Grauerholz's remarks at William's Bardo Burn, September 20, 1997.

> *Why are we here?*

> *Each and every one of us has a different answer to that question, and we can meditate on those reasons while we take part in this event tonight.*

> *It has something to do with our hosts, Wayne and Carol, and I know we all thank them for making this gathering possible.*

> *It has something to do with Lawrence, our community - not the "metropolis" of Lawrence, frankly - but the community that we found when we came here, however many years ago we came here*

... the community that we built here, over the years that we have been here ... the community that we share, now, while we are still here.

And it has something to do with William Burroughs. William lived here for sixteen years, longer than he lived in any other place in his life.

Every time William went out in the town, he always ran into friends; he had friends here, everywhere he went.

And every time he travelled far away, he always came home to Lawrence.

Lawrence was William's home, his final home. He lived here, he lived well here, and he died here.

And we all miss him very much.

Now, I don't know how many of us are Buddhists, and I'm pretty sure there are no more than one or two ancient Egyptians here tonight, but I'd like to say a few words about their belief systems concerning life, and death, and life after death.

The ancient Egyptians postulated seven souls - as William's voice will be explaining for us, in a moment ... three of those souls split, at the moment of the death, the other four remain with the subject, to take their chances with him in the Land of the Dead. But first he or she must cross the Duad, the River of Shit, all the filth and hatred and despair of all human history – then, on the other side, lay down the body, the Sekhu, the Remains, and journey through the Land of the Dead, encountering souls from your own life who have gone before - through a thousand challenges and trials, you try to make your way to the Western Lands ...

The Buddhist belief (I can't do this justice right now, but this is basically it) is that your soul, more or less, is reborn again and again, into new lives. Ideally, you would not be reborn, but escape the wheel and of death and rebirth, into nirvana; but the highest enlightened ones consciously vow to be reborn as many times as it takes for all sentient beings to become enlightened, they sacrifice their opening to nirvana - that is the boddhisattva vow.

The idea is that after physical death, the soul wanders through a spirit region known as the Bardo, re-living past experiences, facing images left over from other lives, other karma - and then, usually after about seven weeks, is re-born - attracted to a male and female coupling, and born again, to suffer again.

We are gathered here tonight to perform a ceremony that is ancient and universal - the burning of objects and images associated with the departed, to symbolize the dissolution of the physical body and its intermixture with all other elements - for example, Native Americans, it was pointed out to me tonight, burn the dead person's belongings immediately after death ...

Now if I haven't waited too late and I can still read this, I'm going to read you some short remarks sent here by David Ohle, and by John Giorno:

First, from David Ohle:

"Sendoff Message to the Soul of Bill

Well now, Bill. They say you've done your Bardo time, and now your SOUL is fixing to head off somewhere.

But look here, baby. We're gonna miss that creaky old soft machine you've been walking around in these eight score and three. We got used to it, you know. Those wise and witty things it said. And wrote. And it must have pumped fifteen tons of lead into the world.

I don't know about souls, my dear. But if you have one (and I know you believed you did), then let's give it the giddyup 'n' go. Shoo!

150

*Everybody say it, "Shoo! Giddyup! Git on,
Bill's soul!"*

And take care crossin' that River of Shit.

*Sorry I ain't there today, my dear, but I
figure when you're talking soul travel, what
the fuck is a few thousand miles? I'm
looking toward Kansas right now. I see
something."*

*And this from John Giorno, and I'll try to
approximate his delivery:*

"You generated

enough compassion

to fill the world,

and now,

resting in

great equanimity,

you have accomplished

great clarity

151

and great bliss,

and the vast empty
expanse

of Primordially pure

Wisdom Mind."

All right. Why are we here?

I mean, in the larger sense ... William had a very
definite answer to that question:

We are Here to Go.

Okay, let's burn it.

REMEMBERING JACK MICHELINE

by Ray Freed

I met the poet Jack Micheline in 1970 in New York City at Dr Generosity's, a saloon at 73rd and Second on the East Side. I waited tables there and helped run a Sunday afternoon reading series and was editor and publisher of the Dr. Generosity Press, which from 1969 through 1972 put out a number of books and broadsides of poetry.

Of all the poets who came through the Doctor's doors, and the list is long and impressive, Jack was the only one who was a full time poet. I mean that's all Jack did: be a poet. He had no regular job, didn't teach, and at the time was sleeping on the subway. For drink and food Jack would take a poem or two in typescript, make copies, staple the pages inside a brown folder, and on the cover write the poem's title with a marker. On the inside there was a cover page with the title and Jack's signature and the edition number, like This Is Copy 3 Of A Limited Edition Of 10 Copies, again written by Jack with a marker. These productions he peddled for a few dollars each in saloons and on the street. Jack called them Midnight Special Editions.

At that time there were several saloons with regular poetry readings, uptown and downtown, The Tin Palace and St. Adrian's among them. Jack always showed up for these events, and always, invited or not, got on stage and recited a piece or two. Never read, always recited. He knew all his poems by

153

heart. Other poets carried briefcases stuffed with paper. Jack carried his poems in his head.

At some point in the early 70s Jack moved out to San Francisco and we kept in touch by mail. In 1975 I was involved in the production of a book of his, *Street of Lost Fools*. I lived in Westhampton and had a studio connected to the garage behind the house, where I drank and wrote and kept the pot belly stove cranked up to 80 degrees. One winter night I ran out of plugs of wood for the stove, there was snow on the ground outside where the woodpile sat, I was shirtless and drunk and dreaming myself in Hawaii. No way was I going to get bundled up to go out in the freeze and get wood, no way. So I fed 30 or 40 unbound copies of Jack's book into the pot belly. The stove glowed. Never has any poet's work given me such immediate satisfaction.

In 1980 I moved back to Hawaii and lost touch with Jack. I got sober and realized the book burning was a terrible thing to do. I had to make an amends to Jack, but I had no idea where he was. So I wrote this poem to him:

> *To The Poet Jack Micheline*
> *On the Occasion of*
> *Another Saloon Reading*
>
> *This ain't no Philharmonic Jack*
> *no high walled box built*
> *to amplify the lack which is*
> *any tight wound string's condition*
>
> *no straight backed hall raised*

*to reassure the greedy fry
that increase of sound
equals the sum of the song*

*no tall structure stuffed
with poached fish eager
to bathe in the gentle rip
of your rough songs.*

*A tavern where no cultured poet
dares lay academic intestines bare
for fear of guts*

*a bar where no thought lives
whose truth is hidden
behind wooly words*

*a saloon where any poem
is only as good as a turn of the head,
quiet vocabulary of the eyes*

*a roomful of strangers
come to drink and
listen each to his own voice.*

*Current poets ripple
in closed schools together
degreed, monied, granted*

*stiff fish listening only
to each other, learning
only from each other*

*and though this tiny pond
passes for the sea of poetry*

155

A LITERARY GENERATION'S LEGACY

here in the big city

you Sir,
scotch and ginger aristocrat
true man of the art whose book
is written on the living heart

though cut by age and passing fashion
you come on Sundays
to read yourself
in this saloon.

Consider this a sonnet on your door.

That was my amends to Jack, a true poet. I never thought I'd see him again. Then one night I got a call from Jack, drinking in a Village bar with the poet Dan Murray who had my phone number. 9 o'clock for me in Hawaii and 3 a.m. for them in New York. It was great to hear Jack's voice again. I got his address and we resumed correspondence. I told him about the books used as fuel and sent him the poem. He told me the burning was okay since I had to keep warm, and said he liked the poem, he was making copies to give out on the streets in San Francisco. Then I was in New York in 1994 and saw Jack on Bleecker Street, we had coffee and he said he was waiting for the limo to take him to the studio, he was taping the Conan O'Brien show. Next day he came out to Riverhead and on to Sag Harbor for a reading at Canio's and we spent the night as guests of a lady poetry lover whose name escapes me and the following day taped a television segment having to do with Street Press, which was the publisher of *Street of Lost Fools*. We had a good time.

Then Jack went back to the West Coast and I went back to
Hawaii. We wrote back and forth until Jack passed away.

I had quite a collection of letters and drawings and paintings
Jack had sent me over the years. I needed to get new teeth so I
sold them as a package to a person who collects things like that.
I got the teeth and felt I should let Jack know about it, that once
again I had used his writing for my personal satisfaction, so I
wrote him this poem:

> *It hasn't changed Jack*
> *they're still whipping the metal flanks*
> *for speed and anybody of worth*
> *has been turned out into the cold.*
>
> *It's coming to a boil again*
> *with new and bigger weapons,*
> *any day now a bright light will dull*
> *the sun and biochemistry lay waste millions.*
>
> *Poetry's a murmur, starved thin*
> *with washboard ribs, living*
> *on the outskirts, taught in college*
> *by mortgages in suits.*
>
> *At least the night is quiet, full of peace*
> *and sleeping birds dreaming dawn.*
> *What's it like there? Is it Paradise*
> *or just another dry mouth morning?*
>
> *I'm selling all your books and letters*
> *because I need new teeth. I know*
> *for teeth or hunger you'd forgive me Jack.*

157

I've got food but nothing to eat it with.

CORSO COLLAGE

(Gregory Corso died on Jan 17, 2001. The following poems and reminiscenses were posted to a Literary Kicks tribute message board in the weeks that followed. Where an author provided a name, the name appears here. Otherwise, the author's chosen message board username is used. – Levi)

I heard your typewriter tore your mind to ribbons.
You, who hated "OLD POET MEN,"
who wanted to "cut out their apology-tongues
and steal their poems"
must have been at your wits end up there in Minnesota,
burning the long end of a 70-year-old smoke,

You, who lingered in the naked shadow of Allen Ginsberg,
spouting Brooklyn-ese in dank apartments,
and treating your women like words,

You, who stared out your snow-globe window
not sure if it was the Northern winter
or the white curtain of drug funk
that clouded your vision

(They said you never came out in public unless you were loaded)

A LITERARY GENERATION'S LEGACY

You, Gregory Corso, are dead.

But it was also You who said
"Death is a rumor spread by Life"
so do me a favor when you reach the angels:
Say hey to Allen, Jack, and Old Bill.
We miss you all.

-- *Beatnik Rooster*

In 1994 I was lucky enough to attend a Beat conference in New York City at New York University, where I had the great fortune to see, hear and meet a great many of the Beat family. Allen Ginsberg, Micheal McClure, Jan Kerouac, Ann Charters, Lawrence Ferlinghetti, Anne Waldman, Carolyn Cassady, and many others. Gregory Corso was one of my favorites for the story he gave me to tell.

On May 21, 1994 the 2nd or 3rd day of the conference I was turning 25. Not having a Corso book handy, I went to him and asked him if he would sign my Canadian passport, hoping he would notice I was 25. He looked at me at said "Passsport, NO!" in his thick nasally New Yorkese accent. Others around laughed, and said that was a good try. Later on during the conference when Ginsberg had us all breathing deeply and meditating Corso was cracking jokes, and he just had far too much energy to sit still even for a few seconds. I will forever remember Gregory Corso, as a great poet with overflowing energy, & a childlike honesty, telling it like it is, like King Lear's fool. Corso

was a clown with all knowing eyes. He said what he saw,
smiling.

-- *pooka*

dress sexy at your funeral
your voice was lavender in sandpaper
you read beautiful poems
and wrote clever ones
to legions of cynical literates
who chose to laugh at the absurd
rather than bother changing it.

you indulged us by writing
about yourself
we wanted to know more
i want to know what i'll be like when i'm twenty five
i want to know what marriage is.

you drew pictures next
to the poems we read
stick figures
crucifixes
happy things
children draw

and you werent particularly innocent
no one said you should be
but you werent cunning

A LITERARY GENERATION'S LEGACY

even as Yuri you were lovable
(though kerouac may disagree...)

so,
disappear
below
the
earth:
where
the
sun
fades
at
summer's
end.

-- *Ted Guastello*

Once upon a time back in the Fifties in Paris Gregory and I went
to small dinner party where we met James (*From Here to
Eternity*} Jones who just arrived in Paris. After dinner Gregory
started bemoaning the fact that he had no place to stay.

A young couple present at the dinner offered him floor room in
their newly renovated apartment while they went on a trip. The
newly white painted walls drove Gregory wild and you can guess
the rest of the story.

-- *Graham Seidman*

Corso's gone,
a noumenon, with this
inauguration's
moon will rise
a midnight's eye
the holy beats called noon -
they Sacajawea'd a time
through themselves: that's
the wilderness Moses faced, the
secret fires and clouds in
there same as what Emily
chased. I'm in love with you
forever Emily and Gregory and
Robinson, but so sad, so sad. Guess
what? Today they stopped
light and the Amazon's
burning. They say that 40%
will be gone by 2020. Why is
this planet happening? Why is
its most beautiful thing bent on
becoming loathsome? It's 'cause
they're scared, we're scared, all's
scared of the mind that it is,
so let's murder freedom some
more. They say 60% of the coral
reefs gone by 2030. I wonder,
Gregory, if on Saturday someone
will pie Bush's face

A LITERARY GENERATION'S LEGACY

and point fingers you
made
pointable at
your life when he goes by but probably not.
Will there be anybody there with a sign that's just
plain empty? America tonight I'll whisper here for you,
America, America, to our world this name's been given, we all
knew you would die like this tonight, but I'll whisper America,
America, tonight here for you, America, I'm not scared to
comfort you and the world tonight, you know who I mean when I
name her, she's the one with the pre-baptized soul, you slipped
on her
in your shower and cracked your teeth out, I thought of her and
you last week
by the ocean, the way you two'd make love, you giving her
nuzzles and kisses while gulls
called god's messages from your happiness and you knew they
were his oh, be with her tonight
as you've never been, pass over the houses and the barns and
the mountains, linger in the moonlight a
few days and I'll whisper our name, you're walking in the stars,
I'll whisper your name, America, America,
I'll whisper her name.

-- lamplighter95501

In 1957 Gregory used to hang out at the Cafe Monaco on La
Place Odeon, which catered mostly to ex-Korean war vets
studying French girls and wine on the G.I. Bill. One day Jack

Stern, a polio-disabled Franco-American playboy pulled up in his chauffeur driven Bentley. Gregory demanded all the money in the Jack's pocket but Jack held out $100 for lunch (he liked to eat well). Gregory argued but settled for what was about another $100.

This was enough money to support Corso for a month but he decided to buy a coat for protection against the coming winter. He went to the flea market and while looking for a coat, he spotted a velvet Hamlet costume which he bought instead. He sat around his attic room in the "Beat Hotel" In his velvet costume ... BROODING!

-- *Graham Seidman*

outside
gregory corso
sleeping under
a maple tree
(or was it aspen,
or pine?
gregory corso
sleeping with
(i think it was
max's mom)
cold, dark,
everyone gone
i found a sleeping bag
(did i steal it?)

165

A LITERARY GENERATION'S LEGACY

gregory corso
looking up with
one eye open---
Thanks sweetie

-- inlieu

After not seeing Gregory for over ten years I was surprised in 1970 to see that most of his teeth were missing. He told me that he went to visit the poet Charles Olsen who was teaching at some university. Since Gregory was penniless as usual he asked Olsen to check into the possibility of the university buying some of his manuscripts.

Olsen agreed to try and told Corso to wait in his lecture room and entertain his students while he talked to the proper person. After a while Olsen returned and loudly informed Gregory that he was able to get $2000 for him. Evidently he did this in a humiliating enough way to piss Gregory off and so he shouted out in front of Olsen's students "Thank you -- you delicious faggot".

That night there was a knock at Corso's motel room door and when he called out "who is it" a girl's voice answered. When he opened the door to admit what he thought was a "groupie" Olsen stepped in and punched him in the mouth, hard enough to knock out most of his teeth. And so it is in the world of poets.

-- Graham Seidman

I remember something like ten years ago Gregory following
Allen into a crowded bookstore before they did a reading --
Gregory in a trench coat and holding a paper shopping bag,
inquiring LOUDLY about Allen's health.

"How's yer heart, Allen?"

Allen, resignedly, "It's fine, Gregory."

Like talking to the kid brother he loved. What a pair.

God Bless You, Gregory.

-- *weepnot*

I never had the honor of meeting Gregory Corso, yet I've read
Jane Kramer's "Allen Ginsberg in America" so many times, I feel
that I knew him: "Allen is my best friend, and I don't even like
him any more ... You know why, Allen? Because you sing bad.
You're always singing. Maretta sings good, Allen, but you don't
sing good."

-- *gbritso*

american hero

A LITERARY GENERATION'S LEGACY

i've got your books
don't worry,
we'll meet
it's predicted by the
tanks and pipes
you turned a 14 year old boy
to a 20 year old dog
who writes about you
thank you,
the army does
-- *irishralphie*

While spending the Christmas holidays with me in Ponce, Puerto Rico in 1970, Gregory expressed a desire to try his luck at the roulette tables at the Intercontinental Hotel. Bizarre as he looked in a borrowed suit two sizes too big and a headful of uncombed and unkempt wild hair, the snooty doormen allowed him to enter this den of playful dollars. After drinking, turning on and gambling all night, Gregory had run the $50 he was saving for a Christmas present for his wife in Colorado into $800. " Man ... now I can afford to buy a ticket and bring the present to her in person" he sang out happily. Wiped out exhausted as I was, I was delighted when he agreed that we should leave instantly. But, on the way out he demanded one more shot at the table. "Double or nothing", he laughed as he placed all his chips on the red and of course the ball dropped into the red and then jumped out again and landed full stop in the black.

"Gregory, you schmuck ... you lost everything your tickets to Colorado, your wife's Christmas present, everything", I lamented.

"No ... Not everything, I'm still alive, ain't I? And that's all that counts" he said. He never mentioned it again.

-- *Graham Seidman*

some dank representative for a doom'd dance senate
in yr business suit of dirt
i'm sure yr death was like yr
poesy

full of choking words
& unstable endings

i've known other men thru their writing, gregorio,
but you have been a hair-raiser from the very
start

&
the beat generation is a sad novella with/out
yr

madcap'd antiquated
heraldry

it's a shame that only the fringe is left to deal

A LITERARY GENERATION'S LEGACY

out shameless cards in hopes of saving some fragment
of

self-esteem
that ends up growing bored & quickly leaves like red
fire trucks leaping out of lips

it becomes
shelf-esteem

i've grown bor'd with words lately
nunzio
but yr death has reawakened some mildew
in the tiles

i saw death under the kitchen sink yesterday
& humility was betting away ego at the horse track

i am a rookie in madness
& an expert in lunacy

you & i, corso, are moonmen
the eagle has landed god

who is the madman this time? get the padd'd room ready

angels evacuate their water-cooler wisdom
god better be waiting

with his sketch pad

you'll have beauty yet i swear
in the form of words that serve as yr headstones
or in nude angels

blushing.

-- *Beatnik Rooster*

My father told me Gregory Corso died yesterday, and i curled up and read him for the evening.

My mother hadn't heard when we spoke today. I told her, and she started crying. Apparently, the first time she ever went to a protest was when SUNY Buffalo wanted to fire him for not signing the anti-communist pledge.

Why is it that only passing cause such connections to occur? My mother cried, I cried, and we haven't cried together since I was very young.

I hope he appreciated it.

-- *Caity Cat*

Goodbye Gregory
I never got to meet
you

A LITERARY GENERATION'S LEGACY

I just learned about your death

10 days after you left

You'll be with your friends now
and all yr other heroes too

Goodbye gregory

I'm sorry if my bad poetry starts to
fill this world

-- *Shagz*

I was told to show up at Our Lady of Pompeii, a Catholic Church
in Greenwich Village, at 9:30 a.m., and that's all I was told.
Stupid me! I didn't realize until I spotted pallbearers walking
down the aisle carrying the heavy coffin that this was not just a
poetry reading/service for Gregory Corso. This was his funeral.
Wow. I would have dressed better. Or at least I would have
thought about dressing better.

It was a wonderfully moving ceremony. The church on Carmine
Street in Greenwich Village is apparently where Gregory was
baptized, and where his mother took him to worship when he
was a kid (back before it was completely hip, Greenwich Village
was a largely Italian residential neighborhood, and this was

172

where Corso was raised). It is a beautiful, ornate and cheerful church. Either by design or by chance, the large back windows of the church are set so that the morning sunlight infuses the entire room with white light.

It was a traditional Catholic service, presided over by the smiling Rev. Joseph A. Cogo, who seemed aware that Gregory Corso's funeral was something special. He spoke some perceptive words about the human right to be a non-conformist, and said something about God giving us freedom to be ourselves, which I wish I could remember. Gregory's close friend Roger Richards delivered a touching eulogy. Patti Smith sang "Nature Boy" with David Amram playing flute, as the Reverend circled Gregory's coffin waving incense.

I wished we could have heard from others in the crowd, like Bob Holman, Ed Sanders, Tuli Kupferberg, Marty Matz, Ira Cohen, Janine Pommy Vega, Steve Dalachinsky, Eliot Katz ... I could go on and on. But this was a funeral, not a poetry reading (as I'd expected it to be) -- and I think there will be a public reading somewhere else in the Village in the next few days.

Leaving the church, I remembered something I'd forgotten up till that moment. At the Whitney Museum's exhibit of Beat Art a few years ago, one of my favorite pieces was a small collage of at least a hundred church steeples, all cut out of photos and glued together into a single arrangement. Gregory Corso was the artist, and I think this was his only entry in the Whitney exhibit. I love art that is small, unique, highly detailed and highly

A LITERARY GENERATION'S LEGACY

unappreciated. "Found Art" ... like Gregory's life. Anyway, I was completely honored to be at his funeral.

-- *Levi Asher*

all sad dreamers pass this way someday
dreaming of dark cafe days –
BUT I remember the first time I read "Howl"
aged 14, anno 1966 & all the coruscating
brilliance of acid flashes or romilar delirium
or or or ... then & since. And Corso and all
the lot of hairy transgressors gave us all the   gift of inspired
loony & gigantic FREEDOM
from Ike's boring whitebread '50s. Thank
God the final accounting's not in yet ... what's
YOUR take?
-- *aiongeo*

At a Christmas party in San Juan, Gregory was introduced to Dona Casals, the beautiful young widow of Pablo Casals.

"I understand you are a poet", she said to him. "Well, make me a poem".

On the spot he said:

"I came to San Juan
and met Dona

174

and I wanna"

-- Graham Seidman

Scared shitless screaming I blazed home to my flaming
suburban gassy dreams glory fame
For my weedless lawn and taunts and torts from my neighbors
rising up to greet me
Fawning fearful falling stumbling in my bermuda shorts
I set the torch myself
On fire at forty I ran I ran I fucking ran all the way home
From a madman who made me guffaw out loud right there in the
jamocha bookstore
Standing next to the diet books and dirty magazines
I shook I shook thrilled by this gum snapping wisecracking
moppy devil bastard
Him and his tales of Kerouacky going poof! into the fatted air
Cracking up I cackled they tried to kick me out the clerks
I cheated threw down the book ran out the door sailed right past
the sitting clerk staggered there on the curb
Twirling dead black roots of blonded hair snarling at me as I ran
past

First
I knew to read one more page would mean that I would write no
more but roar from a throated voice not my own

Second

A LITERARY GENERATION'S LEGACY

I vowed and in my swearing swore to look up this angel commie
barking madman and upon finding him fall down in love and lay
my head upon his lap and hand him twenty dollars

Third
I'd crouch there waiting for every crack and every crumb a gift of
gravity from his mouth I'd catch them all and chew them up and
inside out for all my days of sustenance

Stop

Smell posies

Put down the junk of fame
Lay down
Hallucinate
You are someone else
A friend in name
Stuck in time and in doom

He came in again
Last night in the rain
His hair gone he bemoaned a hirsute fate of a balding pate
Forget about girls he cried, start smoking pipes

And I shrieked!

Lying across a mattress on the floor at dawn
Legs dangling off dumbstruck and in love
Three rosy angels teasing him

176

life death life
never catches up
When he said "I was a poet before the poems came"
I shot straight up
The cracks in my heart many and never the same

Shit
This guy he's too much
And what about all those others
Drowning I looked up at all those gelded shelves
Shipwrecked hosts all lined up for me
And I couldn't even save one soul

Gregory Corso cursing in my veins
Get thine the fuck out of my brain

I tossed my lunch lurching in the library
I bolted wretching running
Man, I just had to

When I came home I turned on the oracle
Flashing beacons striped my face
The spiders told me of his fate
Dead at seventy-one, four months past

Christ, I was too late

His ashes shipped to Italy
In the poet's corner
You will find him there

A LITERARY GENERATION'S LEGACY

right next to Shelley

-- *Jay Meija*

MARTY MATZ

by Laki Vazakas

The poet Martin Matz died in the evening of October 28, 2001 at the hospice unit of New York's Cabrini Hospital. I believe Marty was 67 years old. I met Marty in the Chelsea Hotel in 1989 and we remained close till his dying day. This is some of what I remember him telling me about his life. Because we were usually pleasantly loaded when we talked, some of my memories could be off a bit.

Marty was not a prolific poet, but he was a poet's poet. Marty's poetry was a unique fusion of Surrealism, Lyricism and Beatitude. He was inspired by, and refined, the traditions of vagabond poesy. Look on the back cover of his book Time Waits: Selected Poems 1956-1986 (JMF Publishing, 1987; privately revised and expanded, 1994), and you will find encomiums from the likes of Gregory Corso, Jack Micheline, Harold Norse and Howard Hart. Beat eminence Herbert Huncke wrote a stirring introduction to Matz's book of opium poems, 'Pipe Dreams' (privately published in 1989). Huncke wrote that Matz "... draws support for the solidity of his statements from the earth, the soil – all of nature; trees, rocks and gems – upheaval and restless winds – strange dream-producing flowers. His is an awareness of the endless mystery we are all so much a part of."

Marty was decidedly his own man, and stayed true to his own poetical calling. He wrote poems for himself and for his friends, and did not taste the admiration of a wider audience until late in

179

his life. What quenched Marty's soul was late night pow-wows burnished with jazz, sharing tales of the brotherhood of fringe dwellers. His love of the nocturnal shines through in his masterful poem I KNOW WHERE RAINBOWS GO TO DIE (On The Death of Bob Kaufman):

TOGETHER WE WALKED THROUGH A FABLED CITY
OF HALLUCINATING GREEN
AND TALKED AWAY
A THOUSAND SMOKING NIGHTS
AS YOUR ACHING HEART
BEAT ITS BONES
IN TIME TO BIRD'S BRILLIANT SOUNDS
OVER THE NEON STREETS OF MURDERED SCHEMES

Matz was born in Brooklyn, spent his adolescence in Nebraska, and served in an alpine unit (no mean feat for a flatlander) in Colorado during the Korean conflict. After the service, Marty gravitated to San Francisco, where he studied anthropology and met Jack Kerouac, Neal Cassady, Gregory Corso and Bob Kaufman. Just as he was becoming part of the incipient North Beach poetry scene in the late 1950s, Marty hit the road, heading south.

I AM THE PERPETUAL WANDERER
THE INSATIABLE TRAVELER
THE MYSTIC NOMAD
FOREVER MOVING
TOWARDS SOME STRANGE HORIZON

OF TWISTED DIMENSIONS
AND CHAOTIC DREAMS

(From "Under The Influence of Mozart" by Martin Matz)

His insatiable thirst for travel led Matz to Mexico and South America, where he wandered from the late 1950s through the late 1970s. He told me so many wondrous tales of his meandering in Peru, Chile, the Yucatan. On one of his journeys he ran into the legendary director John Huston. He told of how he and John and several others drank for a solid week, talking through the nights. Marty insisted that Huston never once slurred his words.

Marty was an intrepid traveler, restless, always seeking and finding the least-trodden path. He told me of how he was once bitten by a snake while crossing a river in Mexico. The flesh on his lower leg turned a hideous purple-black, but he kept going. He always kept moving.

Another time he was stricken with a flesh-eating parasite. Doctors told him that his arm would have to be amputated. He sought out a shaman, took a week of yage cures in a longhouse (in which the shaman "threw light" into the darkest corners of night), and successfully avoided any surgical procedure.

Matz became fascinated by pre-Columbian art, and translated an unknown Aztec codex, "The Pyramid of Fire".

A LITERARY GENERATION'S LEGACY

Marty was also an accomplished smuggler, but those are tales to be told at another time. Suffice it to state that National Geographic did a story which elucidated some of his unique talents as an contraband ceramist.

In the late 70s, Marty was pinched in Mexico with some grass and cocaine on him. Because Mexico had signed a treaty with the Nixon Administration which forbid transfers of drug prisoners, Matz's only recourse was to bribe his way into a somewhat inhabitable cell block in the notorious Lecumberi Prison.

Lecumberi was an old, dingy, frightfully overcrowded prison, built by Porferio Diaz in 1903. By his wits, Marty was able to survive four horrific years of the most abominable incarceration. In 1994, he told Huncke and me how he once was sitting in the Lecumberi yard when one man stabbed another in the throat, showering Marty with "a fountain of blood". He said: "I didn't know the human body could pump blood that fast". It was a tribute to Marty's formidable powers of resilience that he chuckled as he emphasized that "I don't like to be showered in blood". Matz's warm and infectious sense of humor always remained intact.

When the Mexican government decided to close Lecumberi and transfer the prisoners to a new facility, Marty and another prisoner hid for days in a tunnel which they had spent months excavating. They hoped the prison officials would eventually stop searching for them. They were finally captured after hiding for a week, and much ado was made of their daring exploits in the hyperbolic Mexican papers. (For more information on Marty's experiences in Lecumberi, I suggest checking out his interview in Romy Ashby and Foxy Kidd's wonderful *Goodie* Magazine, issue number 6).

In 1978, Marty returned to the US as part of a prisoner exchange with Mexico. He settled in San Francisco and once again shared his poetry at readings. He renewed old friendships with the city's poets, including Jack Hirschman, Gene Ruggles and Neeli Cherkovski.

In the late 80s, Marty married film maker Barbara Alexander. They spent the better part of the next eight years in northern Thailand, living on Barbara's inheritance.

Marty and Barbara also spent some of this period in New York's Chelsea Hotel, where they presided over a convivial literary salon. Their Chelsea suite was filled with the lost art of conversation, the walls covered with exquisite artifacts from Thailand, Nepal and Burma. Painter Vali Myers, storyteller Herbert Huncke and poet Ira Cohen were frequent guests. At one memorable birthday party for Matz's longtime friend and patron Bob Yarra, Harry Smith held court. Huncke and Matz gave two compelling readings at The Living Theatre at this time.

In 1991, I traveled with Marty and Barbara to Thailand and Burma. Together, we made a 26-minute video travelogue called "Burma: Traces of the Buddha", which documents a boat ride down the Irrawaddy River, a Shin Byu (coming of age) ceremony in Pagan and the dedication of a new temple in New

A LITERARY GENERATION'S LEGACY

Pagan. Our time spent exploring together was indeed inspiring. After our visit to Burma, I settled with Barbara and Marty in Ban Muong Noi, a small hilltribe village north of Chiang Mai in Thailand. It was in this small, remote village that Marty wrote his book of opium poems, *Pipe Dreams*.

In the late 90s, after having settled in Healdsburg, California, Marty and Barbara separated. Marty again hit the road: Mexico; Vienna, Austria; Italy. He found a warm receptiveness for his poetry in Italy, where he joined a "Beat Bus" tour of poets, including Ira Cohen, Lawrence Ferlinghetti and Anne Waldman. For several readings, Marty was backed by avant-saxaphonist Steve Lacy. Marty stayed for months with friends outside of Rome, where he basked in the glow of recognition of his poetical gifts.

In 2000, Marty found himself back full circle in his native Brooklyn. He recorded a CD of his poetry ("A Sky of Fractured Feathers") with master musicians Chris Rael (sitar, guitar) and Deep Singh (tabla, harmonium). He gave memorable readings, embellished by Chris and Deep's deft playing, at the Brooklyn Museum of Art and the Gershwin Hotel.

Marty was a thoughtful and comforting presence throughout old and dear friend Gregory Corso's valiant final months battling cancer. Gregory affectionately referred to Marty as "my Matzoh Ball". Matz's eulogy for Gregorio was among the most moving at the memorial services for Corso at the Orensanz Foundation and the St. Mark's Poetry Project.

Matz spent his final months at Lower East Side apartment of his longtime friend Bob Yarra. Marty, like Huncke and Corso before him, received a new generation of admirers in a modest, TV-lit abode. He graciously acceded to interviews while drinking cognac and watching his beloved San Francisco 49ers (Marty loved football and the sweet science of boxing). Old friends Roger and Irvyne Richards, owners of the much-missed Rare Book Room, came by to watch the Yankee playoff games. All the while, Marty continued to spin his magical tales of a fiercely uncompromised, hectically picaresque life.

Like his close friends Herbert Huncke and Gregory Corso, Marty Matz stayed true to himself, always traveling, always savoring extraordinary experiences, always sharing freely his unique impressions yet never straying from his chosen, off-the-Beaten poetical path:

> *UNDER A SHADOW OF FRACTURED ECLIPSES*
> *IN THE WINTER'S UNHARVESTED SHADE*
> *IN SOME MARINADED ANGLE*
> *SOME SECRET PERSPECTIVE*
> *SOME HIDDEN TRAPEZOID*
> *SOME MECHANIZED EQUATOR*
> *OR OCCULTED WRINKLE*
> *ON THE INVISIBLE LONGITUDE OF MADNESS*
> *IN MONEY'S FROZEN SMILE*
> *IN EXPLOSIONS OF ENDLESS EXPANSION*
> *IN THE GULLEYS AND CANYONS OF TIME*

> *(From "In Search of Paititi" by Martin Matz)*

A LITERARY GENERATION'S LEGACY

Before he passed, Marty bragged that he was "the laziest man in the world – and getting better at it every day". But like Huncke, Matz was not aware of how giving he was, how generous he was with his time and his tales.

AN INTERVIEW WITH DIANE DIPRIMA

by Joseph Matheny

Since I was young I admired beat literature and its developers. My young mind was taken with the romantic image of Kerouac roaming the interior of the body politic, a mad sweating virus on the loose in the highway vein of Amerika, Ginsberg holy maniac,chanting, praying, exorcising a generation ruined by madness, Burroughs and Gysin, pushing the envelope, rubbing out the word, and DiPrima, conjuring, stradling the magick/dream line, throwing us bits of tasty metamorsels and sumptuous subconcious feasts.

If you're saying to yourself, "DiPrima?" you are one of the main reasons I wrote this article. Even if you have heard of Diane's work you have to admit, in a field that already has an amazing paucity of women, to overlook even one seems like a capital crime, especially this one. Diane DiPrima is a San Francisco writer and poet who works in healing, Magick, and Alchemy. Her more recent books are: *Pieces of a Song: Collected Poems*, City Lights, 1990, *Zip Code*, Coffee House Press, 1992, and *Seminary Poems*, Floating Press, 1991.

I spoke to Diane on September 22, 1993 in her cozy booklined San Francisco apartment. We spoke of rebellion, liberty, conditioning, and on being a women in the Beat Generation.

A LITERARY GENERATION'S LEGACY

Joseph: When you started out as a writer in the 50's, were there a lot of control systems set up to punish anyone who tried to break out the consensus mold?

Diane: It was a weird time. Especially for women. Rebellion was kind of expected of men.

Joseph: When men rebelled they were romantic, free. Women who rebelled were categorized as being nuts.

Diane: Yes. Nuts or a whore, or something. Yes.

Joseph: Do you feel it's any different now?

Diane: Not much. I think there's been a lot of lip service paid to how much women have managed to advance. The younger women that I know are behaving pretty much like women have always behaved. Maybe they don't have so much of the middle class housewife dream, but they'll still be the one to get a job, while the man does the writing or the painting or whatever. I can think of example after example of this. I think that the internal control systems that have been put in place for women haven't been dented. It's such a big step forward to single mom, but so much more could be going on besides that.

Joseph: That's where the most effective censorship and control systems reside, inside ourselves, our heads!

Diane: Yes! How it gets there is interesting too.

Joseph: How do you think they get there?

Diane: I would guess that it starts in the womb. Getting imprinted with the language pattern that's around you. The way people move, the way they hold themselves. To break it you'd have to do some really deliberate debriefing, on every level. The place where I was lucky in my own life was that I had a grandfather who was an anarchist. I didn't see much of him after I was 7 because my parents thought he was bad for me, but from 3 to 7 I saw a lot of him. I was still malleable enough so some debriefing occurred there. He would tell me these really weird fables about the world. He would read Dante to me and take me to the old people's anarchist rallies, and all this showed me these other possibilities ...

Joseph: So you had an early imprint of a kind of ... anti-authority, authority figure. (laughs)

Diane: (laughing) Yes! Aside from being an anti-authority authority figure the imprint that I got from him and my grandmother as well, was of two people who weren't afraid, at least from my child's point of perspective. They would just go ahead and do what they believed in. In all the other years of my early life I never encountered anyone else who wasn't afraid. I think kids today may be a little better off in that they encounter a few people who either aren't afraid, or who will go ahead and try something anyway, whatever it is. There's a possibility of that model, but during my childhood that was a very unusual model. I was born in 1934, during the depression, and everyone seemed to be frozen with terror. We ... will ... do ... what ... we ... are

189

… told! (laughs) And I don't think it's changed that much. Every day people are told that they should be afraid of not having health insurance, they're going to die in the gutter and to be afraid of all these things that aren't threats at the moment. Of course there are present threats but nobody's paying attention to those.

Joseph: It seems to me that rebellion itself has become a commodity; the media has co-opted rebellions like rock-n-roll, Dada, Surrealism, poetry, the rebel figure. Do you feel that this co-option has succeeded in making rebellion somewhat ineffectual?

Diane: No. What you're seeing is an old problem in the arts. Everything is always co-opted, and as soon as possible. As Cocteau used to talk about, you have to be a kind of acrobat or a tightrope walker. Stay three jumps ahead of what they can figure out about what you're doing, so by the time the media figures out that your writing, say, women and wolves, you're on to not just a point of view of rebellion or outdoing them, or anything like that. It's more a point of view of how long can you stay with one thing. Where do you want to go? You don't want to do anything you already know or that you've already figured out. So it comes naturally to the artist to keep making those jumps, that is, if they don't fall into the old "jeez, I still don't own a microwave" programs.

Joseph: Reminds me of a story about Aldous Huxley. When asked if he had read all the books in his quite impressive library he replied, "God no! Who would want a library full of books that they had already read?"

Diane: (laughs) It is true that rebellion is co-opted, but then it always gets out of their hands, it slithers in some other direction. Then they go "oh, how can we make this part of the system?" Like rap. OK, they are co-opting all this regular rap, but now this surreal rap is starting, native tongue, surreal imagery, spiritual anarchism rap, it's not about girls or politics or race and it's starting to happen.

Joseph: Is this something your daughter brings to your attention?

Diane: Yes, I go over once in a while and catch up on what's going on. You see as soon as something is defined, it wiggles off in another direction. I don't think that it's such a big problem in the sense of reaching a lot of people. How does the artist reach a large audience? The people that know are always going to find the new edge, but the mainstream are not that smart or the guy making a top 40 record is not that smart. It often takes them a long time to figure it out. Now that is a problem, because we don't have the time. We need to reach everybody, right away, because we have to stop the system dead in its tracks. It's no longer a question of dismantling the system. There isn't enough time to take it apart, we just have to stop it.

Joseph: Do you feel that there's a somewhat centralized or conscious attempt to defuse radical art or rebellion through co-option or is it just "the nature of the beast", so to speak.

A LITERARY GENERATION'S LEGACY

Diane: I think it goes back and forth. There are times when it's conscious, but not a single hierarchical conspiracy but rather a hydra headed conspiracy. Then there are other times that it doesn't need to be conscious anymore, because that's the mold, that pattern has been set, so everyone goes right on doing things that way. I'm not quite sure which point we're at right now in history. It's so transitional and crazy that I wouldn't hazard a guess. Just check your COINTELPRO history to see an example of a conscious conspiracy to stop us. Other times it was just a repetition of what has gone on before. Like the ants going back to where the garbage used to be. (laughs)

Joseph: Robotic functioning.

Diane: Yes, and it's all in place when the next so called conspiracy comes along, which is very handy isn't it? I wonder how we've made this monster we have here?

Joseph: Okay. Say we stop it dead in its tracks. What then?

Diane: It would be nice to say it's unimaginable, wouldn't that be great. That would be my hope! (laughs) For one thing, we'd have to use the same tables, wear the same shoes longer, read a lot of the same books, maybe for the next few hundred years. Dumps would become valuable places to mine!

Joseph: They already are to me!

Diane: To some people, yes, but not to enough people. Screeching to a halt seems like the only possible solution and I'm not even sure how you would go about it. Of course the good old general strike would be a nice start.

Joseph: As long as we're on the subject of deconstructing, how do you feel about the predominant intellectual fad of post modernism, deconstruction, and the nihilism implicit in these systems?

Diane: Well, when I read that stuff, it's so frustrating. Western thought always keeps stopping on the brink. It never really makes that extra step. It could really do with an infusion of Buddhist logic. At least four fold logic and then what's beyond that. It seems that although it's dressed up in new language, nothing really new has happened in philosophy in the 20th century. Well, maybe not since Wittgenstein. It seems like the same old thing. You know, sometimes when people ask me for poems now, I'll send out poems that have been lying around for years, I don't always have new poems lying around everywhere, and these things that I wrote as cut-up stuff, cutting up each other's dreams in workshops and such. I'll send these out. Everyone seems to be taking them very seriously and publishing them. They think I'm working off of some language theory when actually these are just things I did for fun.

Joseph: What are you doing now?

Diane: I'm working on 2 prose books. One is called *Recollections of My Life as a Woman*. I'm 120 pages into it and

A LITERARY GENERATION'S LEGACY

I'm still eight years old. I'm still dealing with how the conditioning happened. In my generation a lot of it happened with battering, you got hit a lot, and screaming. Your basic conditioning came through abuse, not really different from concentration camps or anything else. I think someday we're going to look back on how we're handling kids at this point in history and wonder how we could treat them such. Like when people say "how could women stand it when people did such and such?" We'll be saying that about the way children are treated.

Joseph: What's the other book?

Diane: The other prose book is called *Not Quite Buffalo Stew*. It's just a rollicking, fun, surreal novel about life in California. It's in the first person, and in the second or third chapter in I found out that the "I" that was the narrator was a man, so that breaks a lot of rules already. The "I" is a drug smuggler named Lynx. There isn't a whole lot of continuity, just whatever scenes wanted to write themselves.

Joseph: Are you using any kind or random/divination systems, i.e., cut-ups, grab bag, *I Ching*, Tarot, coin tossing, etc.?

Diane: Not with this one. This one dictates itself. The system I guess I'm using is that I can't write it at home. It won't happen anywhere that's familiar turf and it likes to happen while I'm driving. So I'll probably head for Nevada at some point and finish it.

Joseph: What do you see in the future for poetry and literature?

Diane: I would like to see authors really use Magick to reach themes. I'd like to see more work coming out of visioning and trance. I'm really tired of reading about human beings! There's all these other beings, I'd like to see a real dimensional jump and I'd like to see people working on the technical problems. Like when you come back from trance or visioning, or drugs and what you can write down about it at that moment. What you can make into an actual piece, we haven't figured it out yet. Yeats certainly didn't figure it out. It's more than needing a new language. There are actual forms we need to find or the forms have to find us, that will hold all that material without trying to make it reductive. The attempts at visionary painting in the 60's and Yeats' last poems show how vision didn't translate into these old artistic forms. Of course taking the raw material and presenting that as a piece doesn't work either. Maybe a blending of vision, word, and sounds can achieve something. We haven't really had time to think about what the computer is. Most of us still think of it as a typewriter, or a calculator. We don't think of it as its own dimension. It has its own medium, possibilities, to bring this kind of material across. I also think about deliberate invocation to find the plane or thing you want to write about.

Joseph: Do you see us as heading into a post-literate society?

Diane: Yes, we might be. I don't think that will stop poetry, in fact it won't stop any of the arts at all. Even if it's oral there may be a split like there was in Europe when there was the written literature in Latin and then there was the oral poems of the singers in the Vulgate. We have that to a degree already with the poetry of the great song writers. Really though, I don't think literate or post-literate really matters. Were cave paintings literate or pre-literate? Did they read those paintings or just look at them? (laughs) Of course the only reason a completely literate society was developed was for thought control, and now that thought control can be done via T.V., etc. it's not really needed anymore. They don't want everyone reading Schopenhauer!

Diane: Everyone needs to remember that they can buy a small press or laser writer, or copy machine, and go home and do what the fuck they please and it will take a very long time for anyone to catch up with them all! No one seems to remember about a few years ago in Czechoslovakia, without access to all this technology like we have here, even with every one of their typewriters registered to the police, they still managed to publish their work! In order to do this they would they would type it with 10 carbon papers to make 10 copies! We are in a situation here in the US where no one can register all the computers, no one can figure out where all the copy machines are. Get one now! Remember we can do it without government money. Government money is poison, take it when you need it, but don't get hooked. We can say what we want. They can't possibly keep up with us all. Real decentralization!

Joseph: That's great, helping people to find their true desires, but do you think that we're so full of false, spectacle manufactured desires that we can no longer identify our true desires?

Diane: I think it doesn't take that long to deprogram false desires. Anyone who knows that they have the desire to know that about themselves, what their true desires are, will find the tools to do it. Drugs, auto-hypnosis, you could also do it by following the false desires until they lead to a dead end like Blake recommended ...

Joseph: Hmmm ... somehow that seems ... very American ...

Diane: Hmmm ... You're right ...

GARY SYNDER AND ENVIRONMENTAL ACTIVISM

by Jamelah Earle

Language as a Tool for Solving the Global Crisis

> *"Hakuin Zenji puts it 'self nature that is no nature
> ... far beyond mere doctrine.' An open space to
> move in, with the whole body, the whole mind. My
> gesture has been with language."*
> -Gary Snyder, Preface to *No Nature*

Can language bring about environmental change? Poet Gary Snyder shows us that it can. He's not only important as a writer about environmental issues, but also as a prototype for modern environmental activism. Because he strives with his writing to redefine the ways in which nature is popularly perceived, he is combating the generations of negative thought and action directed toward the environment. By changing the way people think about the natural world, one can also change the way they act. Therefore, by studying Snyder's writing, humans discover a new way of interacting with the environment.

Gary Snyder is both a Buddhist and an environmentalist, and he's been combining religion and environmentalism in his writing for more than five decades now. Looking at the need to take care of our world through a Buddhist lens isn't a new concept; for many, the mental states Buddhists wish to achieve (loving kindness, compassion, sympathetic joy and equanimity) only not apply to people, but to all beings on the planet. Because of this, the correlation between Buddhism and environmentalism is a natural one: being unkind to the planet and its inhabitants is contrary to the Buddhist path. Snyder's consistent combination of the two themes is important to a modern discussion on the environment. In his writing, he has given us the most important tool of all: the language to frame our thoughts and discourse (and from there, our actions) on nature.

Snyder won the Bollingen Award for Poetry in 1997. Upon giving him the award, the Bollingen judges said:

"Gary Snyder, throughout a long and distinguished career, has been doing what he refers to in one poem as 'the real work.' 'The real work' refers to writing poetry, an unprecedented kind of poetry, in which the most adventurous technique is put at the service of the great themes of nature and love. He has brought together the physical life and the inward life of the spirit to write poetry as solid and yet as constantly changing as the mountains and rivers of his American – and universal – landscape."

This quotation is striking in that it hints at the inherent relationship between Snyder's writing and his environmental activism – that one does not exist without the other. Snyder's poetry, religious beliefs, and his activism are then all related. By reading his poems to find ecological significance, one also finds religious meaning.

Poems

Gary Snyder has a wide, diverse body of work which encompasses a great number of themes, but one that he returns to with especial frequency is that of human relationship with nature. Snyder describes nature as divine, and this goes hand-in-hand with the biocentric nature of his Buddhist beliefs. For Buddhists, seeing the Buddha nature in their surroundings gives the natural world a religious significance. This significance is evident in Snyder's poems.

The poem "Water" originally appeared in *Riprap*, Snyder's first book of poems. The poems reflect the time Snyder spent in Yosemite, as a trail crew laborer laying riprap, the rock pavement put into trails to keep them from eroding. The poem says,

> *Pressure of sun on the rockslide*
> *Whirled me in dizzy hop-and-step descent,*
> *Pool of pebbles buzzed in a Juniper shadow,*
> *Tiny tongue of a this-year rattlesnake flicked,*
> *I leaped, laughing for little boulder-color coil—*
> *Pounded by heat raced down the slabs to the creek*
> *Deep tumbling under arching walls and stuck*
> *Whole head and shoulders in the water:*
> *Stretched full on cobble—ears roaring*
> *Eyes open aching from the cold and faced a trout.*

This poem shows Snyder in the context of the natural world, and the fact that Snyder does not mention his presence until the fifth line of the poem suggests that he is only a small part of the world – not a dominant figure. Nowhere in the poem does Snyder say he has a more important place than any other part of the ecosystem, rather, it suggests that he is an equal. This is demonstrated in the poem's final line, where he ends up face-to-face with a fish.

While this may be a description of a literal event, deeper ecological and religious implications are communicated by the way in which Snyder presents it. The world that Snyder describes in the poem is one in which everything has a place and is important, and suggests that human life is equal to all other forms of life.

Snyder's poem "For All" puts a new spin on the takes the American Pledge of Allegiance. Instead of pledging allegiance to a flag, Snyder pledges allegiance to the land, saying,

> *I pledge allegiance to the soil*
> *of Turtle Island,*
> *and to the beings who thereon dwell*
> *one ecosystem*
> *in diversity*
> *under the sun*
> *With joyful interpenetration for all.*

Creating a new pledge of allegiance is a revolutionary act. Snyder takes the focus off national identity and instead put it on nature. While God is mentioned in the original Pledge of Allegiance, Snyder replaces him with the sun. By doing so, he is shifting the focus from an outside deity onto a natural object. Just as God is seen as an important, life-giving power, the sun can also be seen that way – the lives of plants, animals and humans would be impossible without the light the sun provides. By replacing God with the sun, Snyder says that the ecosystem is a complete and sacred entity unto itself.

It is also noteworthy that Snyder's new pledge of allegiance makes no specific mention of humans. Humans are implicitly referred to in the line, "and to the beings who thereon dwell," but the poem never raises humans above the other forms of life on Turtle Island. Again, this demonstrates Snyder's belief that humans are only a part of the world, and not necessarily the most important one.

A LITERARY GENERATION'S LEGACY

The final lines of the poem "Ripples on the Surface" show an interesting juxtaposition of human civilization and wilderness:

> *The vast wild*
> *the house, alone.*
>
> *The little house in the wild,*
> *the wild in the house.*
>
> *Both forgotten.*
> *No nature*
> *Both together, one big, empty house.*

The house represents the human habitat, but Snyder places it alone in "the vast wild," which suggests that human civilization is only a small part of the world. Snyder further calls attention to this concept by reiterating and restating it in the next stanza: "the little house in the wild". Snyder's view of the human relationship with the natural world is very clear in the last line, in which he calls both the little house and nature "one big, empty house". Everything – human homes and nature – make up one big ecosystem, which we all partake of and live in. Snyder's use of the word "wild" gives the word a different meaning, because, although wildness is often associated with evil, "the wild [is] in the house." Humans are not separate from wildness. Instead, they should embrace it.

However, Snyder's exploration of the human/nature situation does not end with these sentiments. He goes on to say that the house in the wild and the wild in the house have been forgotten. People have forgotten their inherent connection with nature, and do not see that they are only a part of the ecosystem. He also calls the big house of the ecosystem "empty," which suggests that without the recognition of the connection between humans and nature, the ecosystem is "empty" because it lacks the spirit of coexistence which is necessary for it to be full.

In 2004, Snyder published *Danger on Peaks*, a poetry collection that continues the theme of the interconnection of all living things. For example, the haiku "A Dent in a Bucket" –

> *Hammering a dent out of a bucket*
> *a woodpecker*
> *answers from the woods*

– is a snapshot of working alongside an unseen bird. At different tasks in different locations, each is up to the daily work of their lives, neither more important than the other, creating a sense of solidarity and connection?. It's a small moment about a mundane task. But life is a series of moments like these, and Snyder's choice to portray a human and woodpecker both at work reinforces the belief in the importance of harmony within a location among the other creatures who live there.

These four poems, from different stages in Snyder's career, give a sample of his innovative exploration of humankind's place in nature. Each poem takes up issues, and together they serve not only as a portrait of one man's views of nature, but also as a foundation for a new way of dealing with the environment. Snyder's poems go further than merely being *about* environmentalism or spirituality. They shape our outlook so that it becomes one inherently in harmony with the world around us, providing a template for a new sort of life. Therefore, as formerly suggested, Snyder's poetry is not simply writing about activism, it *is* activism.

The Etiquette of Freedom: A Prescription for the Global Crisis

A LITERARY GENERATION'S LEGACY

In 1990, Gary Snyder published *The Practice of the Wild*, a book of essays about human relationship with nature. The first essay, "The Etiquette of Freedom", examines the terms we use to describe nature. Snyder spends a great deal of time defining the terms "nature," "wild," and "wilderness". Snyder moves away from the definitions commonly given to these words in contemporary culture, and proposes a new idea: that freedom is inherently connected with wildness, and humans must learn to embrace them together. He poses the question, "Where do we start to resolve the dichotomy of the civilized and the wild?" This question is important to any extended discourse on Snyder's brand of environmentalism, because he believes that for the global environmental crisis to be solved, humans must reconcile the created gap between their culture and wilderness culture.

Snyder suggests that the foundations for our present social orders are learned from the order found within nature. Therefore, no matter how much we try to disengage from it, we are connected to nature. In his discussion of language, Snyder says that language is something we learn while living, not while being taught. While schooling can teach us the finer points of language, "the power, the *virtu*, remains on the side of the wild". In other words, nature is a fine teacher, and the perception of the necessity of separation of civilization and nature is just that – a perception, and nothing more.

Part of Snyder's discussion includes mention of Hindu and Buddhist figures, who have relationships with animals. He says:

> *In this ecumenical spiritual ecology it is
> suggested that the other animals occupy spiritual
> as well as 'thermodynamic' niches. Whether or
> not their consciousness is identical with that of
> the humans is a moot point. Why should the*

204

*peculiarities of human consciousness be the
standard by which other creatures are judged?*

Here, Snyder suggests that nature is vast, and by applying human perceptions to other species, humans are limiting the world. Therefore, Snyder argues that humans need to view their relationship with nature in a different way – instead of trying to make it fit preconceived notions of the way things "should" be, we should instead leave nature as it is, and live within it. He also tells us that "home" is as big as we want it to be, and we should stop limiting ourselves to our small definition. This would foster a greater feeling of connection with – rather than isolation from – the natural world.

Snyder concludes his essay with a proposal of how humans should live within the world. He says that if we stop fighting nature, "we can accept each other all as barefoot equals sleeping on the same ground". With that, we can return to wildness at its simplest meaning.

In order to change the way we act toward nature, we have to change the way we think about it, and Snyder's reevaluation of the language we use to describe nature is a fundamental step toward that goal. Taking words that commonly have negative connotations and casting them in a positive light is a basic but necessary part of reshaping our approach to nature: it gives us the vocabulary for a positive environmental ethic. This supports the idea that Snyder's use of language is his primary activist tool. By redefining contemporary notions of nature, Snyder is able to propose a new way of living within the world, one in which environmentally sound habits become the obvious way of life.

Conclusion

205

A LITERARY GENERATION'S LEGACY

Snyder's career has thus been based on writing about nature in ways which are often foreign to the dominant cultural discourse, and his commitment to this presentation of nature is instrumental in shaping modern environmentalist thought. While much of his writing is not explicitly religious, the connection he has had with Buddhism for the greater part of his life is implicit in all of his work.

Although Snyder has been involved in environmental activism in what some may call a more "active" approach, I would like to argue that his body of writing is his most active form of activism. Presenting the issues through writing is important because it gives people the ideas to work from. Without written commentary, "active activism" is not complete.

Language can be a revolutionary tool, and writers and their works have been instrumental in shaping society for generations. Gary Snyder's poetry is part of a long tradition of literature as an agent of social change.

He's not only important as a writer about environmental issues, but also as a prototype for modern environmental activism. Because he strives with his writing to redefine the ways in which nature is popularly perceived, he is combating the generations of negative thought and action directed toward the environment. By changing the way people think about the natural world, one can also change the way they act. Therefore, by studying Snyder's writing, humans discover a new way of interacting with the environment.

AN INTERVIEW WITH ROBERT CREELEY

by Jamelah Earle

Robert Creeley is known as a Black Mountain Poet (along with Charles Olson and Denise Levertov), the Poet Laureate of New York State and a professor, but most importantly, he is a writer with a unique perspective on what's happening in literature today. In early 2004 I interviewed him about community, online writing, spoken word poetry, and finding an audience. Here's what he has to say:

Jamelah: What kind of role do you think writing and connecting with a community of like-minded artists plays in shaping an artist's perspective and style? Is it important? Does it have a downside?

Robert: I think it's extremely important not just for the sake of political action, say, but for all circumstances of a writer's literal life. Company is what keeps it all together – those "few golden ears" Allen Ginsberg speaks of for whom, he says, "Howl" was written. It matters immensely that someone is listening, can hear, knows where you're coming from. The general audience, the wider audience as one says, comes years later, so, as in jazz, it's the people who work with you and give you the necessary feedback who matter. If this can have a downside, it's only in some sad possibility that what said company is after is not particular to writing itself. For example, a friend used to say of his first wife, "She said she wanted to be a singer but what she really wanted was to be famous ..." A company having that so-called goal in mind gets to be a distraction instantly.

Jamelah: Your *Day Book of a Virtual Poet* uses writing originally produced in an online medium (e-mail) to offer its insights, yet it is published in book form. Though online publishing does not currently have the same validity as traditional print publishing, do you think it will someday? Should it have the same validity?

Robert: In that case a small press (Spuyten Duyvil) asked me for something and I thought those accumulated "letters" would be apt. So they proved, and that book has had a remarkable and continuing life. The thing was that the work online depended on Buffalo's high school, City Honors, keeping the material up on its website, and just now checking, I see it's long gone. (All that I found was the note written when Allen Ginsberg had just died.) In any case, it's what simply and cheaply can keep texts and all the uses of them one can think of available, can get and keep work in print. In the 40s, when I was coming in, the absolute limit was letter press and it was awful. No cold press – only ditto, mimeo and such as resource – which one used as did Diane di Prima and Amiri Baraka's "Floating Bear" or as the Golden Goose Press did with its magazine and chapbooks for a time. What a relief to have both distribution AND initial "printing" now be so old time easy! Whatever "validity" constitutes, that has got to mean something in itself.

Jamelah: In terms of poetry, can you think of an example of something the online medium made possible that would not have been possible in print?

Robert: For me it's been the chance to have art specific to something I wrote be there so simply. Here's an instance:

http://www.2river.org/2RView/2_2/poems/creeley1.html

This was done initially as a catalog for a show of Francesco Clemente's and so few people got to see it. This way at least some sense of it is easily available. Note too that it's been 'up there' since 1998 although the magazine it's in has since moved first to Florida and then to the west etc etc. (It began as an online journal out of Damien College in Buffalo.) Anyhow my use of the possibilities is obviously minimal. Think of hypertext – or 'e-poetry' – as you'll find it here:

http://epc.buffalo.edu/e-poetry

I.e., look at the range and action! Really, it all goes on and on. Check out the ubu.com site, for example – it's like a miracle, to be able to hear and see such a range of material – click, click, click! Had anyone ever told me such would be possible in the 40s, it would have been almost impossible to believe.

Jamelah: In the past couple of years, the blog has become an important format on the Internet, and due to its popularity, people who may never have written or shared writing otherwise are publishing their thoughts on the web for the world to see. It seems that everyone has a blog these days. What do you think of this phenomenon? How do you think it changes the notion of what it takes to be a writer?

209

Robert: I much like the quickness of exchange (for which read "publication") it provides. I truly think the more, the merrier – and let one's own perceptions and needs make the relevant connections. Pound said years ago, "Damn your taste! I want if possible to sharpen your perceptions after which your taste can take care of itself." It's as if someone has finally opened that bleak door of usual discretion and habit, and let in a great diversity of response, proposal, everything. Two blogs I value indeed:

http://thirdfactory.net
http://jonathanmayhew.blogspot.com

And one could go on and on (e.g., to Chris Leydon etc).

Jamelah: Though poetry has always had a small audience, things like spoken word/performance poetry and hip-hop are increasing poetry's reach, especially to the young. Do you see this as a positive thing? What do you think of the difference between spoken word and written poetry?

Robert: For me sound – Pound's "Listen to the sound that it makes" – has always been a crucial factor. That's why jazz back then in the mid-forties was so useful – it let me hear ways of linking, how 'serial order' might be played, what a rhythm could literally accomplish. I wasn't getting that from the usual discussions of poetry at all. Anyhow I write and read my own poems as sounds and rhythms – and that is a crucial part of their fact. One gets phrasing from all manner of sources, people talking in the street, Frank Sinatra, and so on. Jack Kerouac is a terrific instance albeit he hardly took to the stage with any pleasure. But anyhow I write poetry to be spoken, I speak it when I write it – like Bud Powell playing piano.

The only question I'd ever have, then, about performance is whether or not it begins to drift to that earlier point of my friend, "She said she wanted to be a singer ..." I have no interest in poetry imagined as a pure art, say, but I don't want it only so as to see one's name in lights either. It's it – and that's the point. What one can do with it is always something else.

Jamelah: What advice would you give to today's young writers (the self-published chapbook poets, the novelists who can't find publishers for the finished book sitting in their top desk drawer, the 18-year-old poet trying to decide if it's worth it to go to college) who want to reach an audience?

Robert: It may well sound too easy to say, but I'll say it anyhow – find your own "golden ears", your friends and locating company, and make your way as that interaction. The so-called world at large is just a lot of particular places and you begin where you happen to be. Being a writer is blessed in that one doesn't have huge canvasses to carry about or have need for ultimate equipment or other musicians so as to make the composite sounds in mind. You can also find simply an endless resource of what's been done, what's can be model, in libraries, online, you name it. Google ho!

A LITERARY GENERATION'S LEGACY

Anyhow I think of Levi Asher and the initial Litkicks – and many friends, Alex Trocchi, Cid Corman, way back then in the early 50s. Who can wait to be tapped? Onward – and good luck!

THE SIX GALLERY: WHAT IT MEANT

by Michael McClure

(I asked poet Michael McClure, one of the five performers at the seminal 1955 Six Gallery poetry reading, if he had any thoughts to share on the event's 50th birthday. He sent me some notes that he planned to deliver at HOWL REDUX in San Francisco's Herbst Theater on the anniversary night. "The first half will be a celebration of earlier San Francisco revolutionary writers – the second half is to honor the Six Gallery readings with revolutionary young poets reading for the original Six readers. I'll read for myself THE DEATH OF 100 WHALES, MYSTERY OF THE HUNT, POINT LOBOS:ANIMISM and NIGHT WORDS. Sandinista Daisy Zamora will read for Philip Lamantia, Leslie Scalopino will read for Philip Whalen and Peter Coyote will read for Kenneth Rexroth." Here's what Michael had to say about the original event. – Levi)

Allen Ginsberg and I first met at a party for W. H. Auden in 1955; Auden had given a reading at the San Francisco Museum and Allen and I were outrageously out of place at a party of academics in a wood paneled old house on Parnassus Hill. Being the wallflowers of the evening, Allen and I soon began talking about our dreams and visions of William Blake, and we made a date to get together for coffee.

After that we often met in North Beach to discuss poetry and the scene. On October 7th, fifty years ago today, we gave our first

213

poetry reading together at the Six Gallery alongside Gary Snyder, Philip Whalen, and Philip Lamantia. It was the first time I met Jack Kerouac who was in the audience shouting "go" as "Howl" had its first reading. Jack collected change between poets and went out for gallon jugs of homemade red wine which were passed through the audience.

The Six Gallery was a space converted from an automobile repair garage on lower Fillmore Street below Union. The young painters in the cooperative gallery were all as outcast as the poets they gave space to for a reading. The painters, now famous, were Jay DeFeo, Manuel Neri, Joan Brown, Bruce Conner, and many others. It was the time of HUAC, Joe McCarthy, the bitter cold war, conformism, silence – and the repression was caging America. There was a Daddy Warbucks martial law on the landscape: a nation of racial segregation,crew cuts, gray suits, tract homes, and Buicks with nose rings.

Kenneth Rexroth, of the older generation of radicals, was one reason the poets were there that night. We had learned much at Rexroth's evenings at home – about California nature, anti-politics, and that we were closer spiritually to the rest of the Pacific Rim, to China and Japan, than to New York. Rexroth was the evening's master of ceremonies.

We were all sick of the drabness of conformist, military America beginning its series of bloody massacres in Asia. The fear and unwillingness to speak, as well as the threat to any who did speak out, was chilling. The young poets that evening were each radicals of their own stripe –from left-socialist, anarchist,

IWW-wobbly to Zen Activist. We knew that poetry was dead –
killed by lacklove and the academies, and each of us wanted to
bring it to life again. And to speak out into the void.

An audience of radical workers, bohemians, artists, and an
earnest professor or two, along with the intelligent-dissatisfied
and some grinning cynics and hopeful idealists showed up to
listen to us and we seemed to present their own thoughts on
stage for the first time. The audience standing or sitting,
crowded in the space, occasionally shouted back their
encouragement or a joke or an acclamation. Most people there
knew that the poets were standing on the ground that had been
cleared by San Francisco's Liberation Circle of outspoken
thinkers and activists and that it could only happen here.

By the end of the evening, following Gary Snyder's deep ecology
poem "A Berry Feast" and Allen's "Howl" – a poem about the
possible new nature of society – we knew we were standing with
our toes against a line in the sand and, whether we felt fear or
exuberance we were staring directly at the wall of censorship
and repression – and we knew we would not step back.

After that evening Kerouac wrote his novel *Dharma Bums*, which
was his turn-about from *On the Road* and into the mountains
and nature. We were all speaking of the new nature. The poems
we read that night had no precedent. It seemed later that we
were not only revolutionary speakers but the also the early
literary wing of the birthing environmental movement. Soon
there was a swift step to the counter culture and its resistance to
Vietnam and the birth of new protest, and to the growing crowds

of activists and action philosophers. In our hearts we believed the evening would become part of the history that mattered to us and that human bodies had been thrown against the wall of obstinate bitter repression, and that things both new and very old were going to begin. A few months later we repeated the reading in Berkeley and things were happening.

I want to thank the audience of that night and the people today who still read the poems from that evening. Let us attempt to protect all living beings of ocean, forest, and city. And life and light to all.

WHEN HIPPIES BATTLE: THE GREAT W. S. MERWIN/ALLEN GINSBERG BEEF OF 1975

by Levi Asher

When I heard that W. S. Merwin had received the 2005 National Book Award for Poetry for his book *Migrations*, I couldn't help but think back to the first time I'd heard his name. We don't often hear stories about distinguished nature poets that involve fist fights, broken bottles and nudity, but W. S. Merwin was the center of an astonishing incident at a Tibetan Buddhist seminar that descended into just such debauchery. The controversy that followed has been largely forgotten, but it occupied the poetry community for several years in the late 70's, pulling the likes of Allen Ginsberg, Robert Bly, Kenneth Rexroth, Ed Sanders, Ed Dorn and Tom Clark into its vortex.

It all went down at a seminary associated with the Naropa Institute, a Tibetan Buddhist outpost in Boulder, Colorado, which hosts the Jack Kerouac School of Disembodied Poetics, founded by Allen Ginsberg and Anne Waldman. The head of the Naropa Institute in 1975 was the charismatic teacher Chogyam Trungpa Rinpoche, whose most famous disciple was Allen Ginsberg. Because of Trungpa's exalted reputation, there was a waiting list for his interactive lectures and training sessions, and apparently W. S. Merwin pulled some strings (he was already at that time a well-connected poet) to get an invitation for himself and his girlfriend, Dana Naone.

217

It seems their desire for special treatment annoyed Trungpa (who had a reputation for unpredictable and impulsive behavior). Trungpa also seemed to bristle when Merwin and Naone expressed strong opinions about the content of the Hinayana, Mahayana and Vajrayana Buddhist source materials, objecting especially to the bloody war imagery in some of the traditional Tibetan Vajrayana chants. Trungpa did not believe a trainee should talk back to a guru, even if the trainee was a celebrated poet.

The Naropa group threw a wild Halloween party, and Trungpa presented a twist: the poets, trainees and other attendants would celebrate Halloween not by putting on costumes but by being stripped of them. The guru, apparently drunk on some sort of spiritual libation that probably did not come from Tibet, walked around the party floor pointing at partygoers, and when he pointed at somebody his assistants would pounce on that person and strip off their clothing. "Chop them up," he would say.

However, Merwin and Naone, having scoped out the scene, made the strategic decision to hide in their room. Trungpa noticed this and sent for them, but they refused to join. Trungpa then sent a larger contingent to retrieve them, this time with the message that they were ordered to join the party. Merwin and Naone, again, refused. At this point Trungpa declared to his faithful attendants that they must use whatever force was necessary to retrieve the wayward guests.

It may be difficult to picture a mob of half-naked, half-costumed hippie Buddhist poets forcing their way into another poet's private room by breaking windows and smashing down doors, but I urge you to picture this, because sources state this is

218

exactly what happened. Apparently Merwin tried to pull a Clint Eastwood move by breaking a bottle and using the jagged remains as a weapon, and all accounts state that several of the scufflers ended up with bloody limbs (though, thankfully, there were no life-threatening injuries).

Finally, Merwin and Naone were dragged screaming and crying into the party, where Trungpa yelled at them, strangely singling out Naone, a Hawaiian, for failing to respect her Asian heritage by following his direction. At his command, the mob descended upon Merwin and Naone and removed their clothing, leaving them naked and sobbing in each other's arms in the middle of the room.

The story ends at this point, and the controversy begins. Naone had shouted for somebody to call the police during the horrific incident, but for some strange reason Merwin and Naone did not immediately leave the seminary grounds, choosing instead to stay several more days for Trungpa's remaining lectures (which indicates that they were probably traumatized and humiliated beyond their better judgement at the time).

Slowly, other poets began to shout for justice, among them Robert Bly and Kenneth Rexroth, who called Trungpa an obscene fraud. The Naropa Institute's funding from several non-profit sources, including the USA's National Endowment for the Arts, was threatened. Allen Ginsberg had not been at the party, but as the spokesman for Naropa's poetry school, a well-known follower of Trungpa and everybody's good friend, he quickly became a central figure in the controversy.

Ginsberg was asked to repudiate Trungpa, his guru, and he would not do so. In various interviews, he repeatedly tried to find the words to defend his teacher's actions, and continued for years to try to walk the line between both sides in this difficult battle.

Trungpa's reputation never fully recovered from this debacle, though he remained active as a religious teacher and activist for Tibetan independence until his death in 1987. Dana Noane continued to write poetry, and edited a volume of modern Hawaiian poetry, *Malama*, in 1985.

Although the strange incident between Trungpa, Merwin and Naone was covered in Harper's Magazine and The Paris Review and is discussed in Barry Miles' biography of Allen Ginsberg, the story has slipped from notice in recent years, despite W. S. Merwin's rising stature as a major voice in American poetry has continued unabated.

Certainly both law and rationality side with Merwin and Naone in this battle, but it's a story that makes nobody look good. Merwin comes across as a Buddhist dilettante, pulling for special favors at a religious retreat, refusing to follow the teacher's commands, and then failing to stand up to the teacher after the horrific treatment at the Halloween party. He made one public statement about the controversy in 1977:

> *My feelings about Trungpa have been mixed from the start. Admiration, throughout, for his remarkable gifts; and reservations, which developed into profound misgivings, concerning some of his uses of them. I imagine, at least, that I've learned some things from him (though maybe not all of them were the things I was 'supposed' to learn) and some through him, and I'm grateful to him for those. I wouldn't encourage anyone to become a student of his. I wish him well.*

Merwin's National Book Award honor in Manhattan came almost exactly thirty years after the Naropa bash that went out of control. According to all reports from the Award ceremony, everyone's clothes stayed on.

DAVID AMRAM TALKS ABOUT MUSIC

by Bill Ectric

In December 1957, jazz musician David Amram and Jack Kerouac improvised a performance at the Brata Art Gallery in New York City that is now remembered as the first Beat jazz poetry reading. Amram has since collaborated with the likes of Gregory Corso, Leonard Bernstein, Willie Nelson and Charles Mingus. This interview explores his ideas about music, and turns up some interesting perspectives on the Beat life along the way.

Bill: How would you explain the term "orchestral colors"?

David: One of the first people who ever spoke to me of orchestral color was Charlie Parker, in 1952, in my basement apartment in Washington, D. C. Parker asked me if I had ever checked out the music of Frederick Delius.

I said, "Bird, we were always told Delius was a minor composer", because in those days, there was a lot lacking in American music studies, and most music teachers referred to Delius that way.

Bird said, "Check out his orchestration. Frederick Delius was a great orchestral colorist."

Bill: But what does that mean?

David: Orchestral colors and the art of orchestration is like taking a series of black and white illustrations and filling them in with colors. In symphonic music, those black and white images are the actual notes played; how and who plays them is what you do when you orchestrate something. A composition is like a great painting in that it has contrast, form, takes you to places you've never been before, and keeps you wanting more.

Bill: What was Charlie Parker like?

David: Charlie Parker had brilliance and sophistication that the movie Bird didn't capture. He was very knowledgeable and he was a lifetime student of 'hang-out-ology', always learning, open-minded, so he didn't rank Delius as a "minor" or "major" musician. He heard the music of Delius for what it was. I talk about this in my book *Vibrations*.

Bill: Your song about Hunter S. Thompson, on the *Southern Stories* CD, is perfect. It captures Thompson's life story so simply and yet, so completely. Did you ever meet Hunter?

David: Yes, I first met Hunter in 1959. I had a cabin in Huguenot, New York when Hunter Thompson was a reporter for the Middletown Daily Record. There was a little store I went to for my week's supply of groceries, and the old man who ran the store hardly said a word, usually just a grunt for 'hello.'

But finally, one day, the guy said to me, "I've seen 'em."

"Seen what?" I asked.

223

"The saucer people", he says. "The flying saucer people in the field across the street."

"Oh ..." I said. "Okay ..."

He said, "I've only told two people about this. You, and that crazy writer up on the hill."

Of course, the crazy writer was Hunter Thompson. Years later, when Ron Whitehead and Doug Brinkley organized an award ceremony for Thompson in Louisville, Kentucky, they asked me to be the music director. I had the chance to sit and reminisce with Hunter about the guy in the Superette who saw the saucer people and other, more serious things, as well. Hunter was more than just a crazy Gonzo character, he was first and foremost a serious writer.

Bill: There is another song on *Southern Stories*, "Alfred the Hog", where you play a flute solo that knocks me out as much as any electric guitar solo. At one point, it sounds like you are playing two flutes at the same time.

David: Thank you, thanks a lot. That instrument is actually an Irish pennywhistle, and yes, on part of the solo, I'm playing two pennywhistles at the same time.

Bill: How did you learn to do that?

David: It just came naturally.

Bill: That figures ...

David: The pennywhistle is a versatile instrument. Just as a violin can be used for either classical or bluegrass, the pennywhistle can be used different ways. Audiences in Kenya enjoyed it when I went there for the World Council of Churches and played African music in 1976. Dizzy Gillespie dug how I used the pennywhistle as a jazz instrument when I played with him in Havana in 1977.

Bill: You composed the soundtrack for the original version of *The Manchurian Candidate* in 1962. I read that Frank Sinatra, the star of the movie, was very pleased with the score you created for that movie. Did you meet Sinatra?

David: I met him in New York a few years after making the film. He said he liked the fact that I'm a jazz musician as well as a classical composer, and he was impressed that I write my own music, orchestrate every note myself, and don't use ghost writers.

Bill: Frank Sinatra, Jr. said that the *Manchurian Candidate* score was an "ingenious combination of polytonality and jazz". Can you explain what "polytonality" means?

David: Polytonal means using more than one harmonic pattern, or two separate tonal bases at the same time.

A LITERARY GENERATION'S LEGACY

Bill: Yeah, Google says, "Using more than one key or tonality simultaneously", but I still don't quite understand it. I play guitar and I thought you could only play in one key at a time.

David: Well, for example, you can play a G7 chord and play a D flat against it.

Bill: No doubt, you can. I'll have to work it. Moving on, I have to ask you this, because there's a debate going on among some friends of mine. You know that famous black & white photo of Gregory Corso, Larry Rivers, Jack Kerouac, you, and Allen Ginsberg, all sitting in the diner? Is that a spoon or a toothpick you are chomping on?

David: I think it was a spoon, as I used to eat yogurt there, but I really have no idea.

We didn't know that the picture was being taken and it certainly never occurred to us that 48 years later, it would be on the cover of books, in articles, museums, and so on.
We were all smiling and having a good time, laughing and enjoying each others company, NOT a bunch of surly hating "Beatniks" as the Beats are sometimes portrayed.

Bill: It looks like a fun group.

David: None of us had on the "costumes" that Beat people were supposed to wear. There was no such thing as a "Beat movement." We were all a group of friends hanging out. Especially Kerouac!

Bill: Who was the little kid who played music with you in *Pull My Daisy*?

David: The kid was Pablo Frank, Robert Frank's son. A great little guy. All this is in my book *Offbeat: Collaborating with Kerouac*.

Bill: Did you ever meet William S. Burroughs?

David: Yes, many times.

Bill: I wondered why Burroughs was not in *Pull My Daisy*.

David: He was not what you would call a gregarious, fun guy. He was fun to listen to when he was talking but he was a very private person.

Bill: I saw you on MySpace recently. What are your thoughts on the Internet?

David: My kids got me onto MySpace. Thanks to the Internet, the generation of my kids have access for the first time in history to all that magnificent music from all around the world as well as the United States. A gifted army of people, who never get played on the radio and whose CD's you can never buy in record stores, now have a level playing field.

You know, the huge record companies are merging in a last desperate attempt to control the listening habits of people all over the world. But with the web and new means of broadcasting, we are now all pardoned from the solitary confinement of the penitentiary of the globalized entertainment industry. My own kids actually draw audiences for their music on the Internet without being part of the music industry. Conversely, a lot of the more obscure stuff I've done can now be downloaded. Right now, you can go to YouTube and find *Pull My Daisy* with Italian subtitles!

As artists, we want to share what we do with others. Of course, we have to pay our rent, buy clothes, take our kids to the dentist, so we have to pay bills. That doesn't mean you have to ruin your art by trying to become a millionaire in two years.

Now, in baseball, a batter won't run out an infield grounder. A basketball player won't make an assist and only want to score points. These players have been forced, by bad advice, to represent what is wrong in their world rather than what's right.

That's why I like playing Farm Aid. Willie Nelson and everyone else at Farm Aid share certain traits: Love of music, caring about other people, inspiring others, and a genuine love and respect for the audience. As a result, all of them are fun to be with.

Bill: Man, you really do play all kinds of music with all kinds of people.

David: Anybody can learn to play any style on whatever instrument they play. You just need to be patient, humble yourself to be with those who know more, and learn the basics.

It's a lifetime job. It's like learning different dialects. Second generation Cubans, for example, have a different kind of Cuban accent than their parents. In the same way, music changes from generation to generation.

Bill: Do you ever compose in your head without score paper?

David: Oh, yeah. Sure.

Bill: Do you ever think something will sound good until you hear it played, and then decide you need to change it?

David: Not really. By the time I get it on paper, it's pretty much right as far as the combination of notes. I may decide to change the tempo or things of balance, like soft or loud, to make it work the best.

Bill: Do you ever see musical sounds as geometric shapes?

David: No, I just hear it very clearly.

PHILOMENE LONG: POET OF VENICE BEACH

by Levi Asher

I met Philomene Long last year at a poetry reading at the Vox Pop coffeehouse in Brooklyn. I knew of her as a veteran of the Venice Beach, California beat poetry scene and as a filmmaker whose documentary *The Beats: An Existential Comedy* I once reviewed (favorably) at Litkicks. Onstage at Vox Pop, she had a healthy ferocity that reminded me of Anne Waldman, and a strong artistic/spiritual core that reminded me of Patti Smith.

I talked to her afterwards about the ongoing Los Angeles poetry community, about her memories of her close friend Charles Bukowski, and about her very cherished memories of her husband and fellow Venice Beach scenester/poet John Thomas (with whom she'd co-authored an affectionate portrait of their mutual friend, *Bukowski in the Bathtub*). I was already captivated by her confident personality, and the sense of poetic self-assurance that she radiated. I was especially fascinated when she revealed an unusual fact: before she became an enthusiastic fellow-traveller with the poets and hippies of Southern California, she had been a Catholic nun.

I had to know more about this, and luckily she allowed me to initiate an email interview after she returned home to California. Meet Philomene Long:

Levi: You are the first poet I've ever met who's once been a nun. In fact, I think you are the first person I've ever met who's once been a nun. Can you tell me what drove you to make such dramatic life choices?

Philomene: Beatitude drove me. In Jack Kerouac's words: "It is because I am Beat, that is, I believe in beatitude and that God so loved the world that he gave his only begotten son to it ... Who knows, but that the universe is not one vast sea of compassion actually, the veritable holy honey, beneath all this show of personality and cruelty?"

I made most of my unique and dramatic life choices before age 8. The first (that I recall) was to sit still.

At age 4: "I will sit!" in a backyard with a woman I called "Miss Aunt Whistle" (because she whistled) and she saying to me: "Sit still, and a small gold bird will come." I chose to sit so still and for so long until I could see every blade of grass, to sit bone quiet, until finally disappearing into a luminosity. And a small gold bird did come.

At age 5: "I will never take my head off my mother's lap!" In church – the sound of her gentle Irish tones saying, "God loves you. God loves you. God loves you" with her hand softly stroking the long strand of my hair. The smell of the pews, the incense. I never wanted to take my head off her lap. And, in some ways, I have not.

Then, at age 7: "I will become a Saint like you, St. Theresa. I WILL BECOME A NUN!". At age 8, finally after writing my first poem in memoriam to my deceased pet duck ("Remember the Day You Were Just Out of Luck"), I became a poet.

Levi: What do nuns and poets have in common?

Philomene: They live as skinless ones. No insulation. Stripped. Utterly naked. Nuns live lives of dedicated poverty.

In fact the first vow all nuns take is the vow of poverty. The first "Beatitude" (for nuns as well as all Christians) is: "Blessed are the poor in spirit for theirs is the kingdom of heaven." John Thomas, my husband, said: "I have Philomene, a pen, a pad, shirt and pants." If you start wanting more, it fills you up, leading to a poverty of the heart and mind.

Buddhism is the religion of the Beats, but many of the Beat writers were Buddhists without leaving Catholicism. Keroauc said every night before he went to sleep he prayed to Buddha, Christ and Mary. Kenneth Rexroth was both Buddhist and Catholic, and was instrumental in bringing poetry and philosophy of the East to the West. Philip Lamantia returned to the Catholic church. I recall him saying his influence was St. Francis, the saint of poverty.

Levi: And how does Catholicism inform your life today?

Philomene: The church that burned John of Arc to the stake for dressing like a man is not the church that canonized her. The

232

church that imprisoned St. John of the Cross on suspicion of heresy is not the one that made him a "Doctor of the Church".

As a child my life was informed by the "Little Way" of St. Theresa of Liseiux; as a young adult by the way of St. Francis of Assisi who stripped naked, and vowed poverty.

The Catholicism that informs my life today is: Pope John XXIII Catholicism; Thomas Merton Catholicism, Dorothy Day Catholicism, Catholic Workers Catholicism and Martin Sheen Catholicism; the murdered Jesuits of El Salvador Catholicism; the anonymous nuns all over the world at this very moment on their knees in prayer or bent over the dying in Calcutta; nuns comforting the mourning at Holy Cross cemetery in Culver City; the nun shot down to bleed out alone on the ground for protecting trees Catholicism; the Jesuits who went to Japan and became Zen masters; the anonymous author of the "Cloud of Unknowing" Catholicism.

Levi: As a Catholic, how do you think difficult issues like abortion rights, euthanasia etc. can be resolved in our country?

Philomene: Within Catholicism? Or generally? I firmly believe in separation between church and state. In no way should they overlap. It is the foundation of our country.

As for within Catholicism ... it's an enormously complex institution. Catholicism is not a one cell being, an amoebae, a planarian. It is a complex entity with – although this seems

233

contrary at first glance – a foundation of democracy. At the same time it exercises the divine right of kings.

Within the church there are many divisions. There are Catholics for Free Choice (e.g. pro-abortion rights), and there is the ARCC ("Association for the Rights of Catholics in the Church") and the WOC (Women's Ordination Committee) – as well as Opus Dei, a group that would return the church to medieval times, including the practice of flagellation.

Personally, I do not speak for any institution. I support Catholics for Free Choice, ARCC, and WOC. As for the center, the Great Heart – a phrase from Thomas Merton runs through my mind: "The seemingly boundless source of sanctity within the Catholic Church."

I am a Zen Catholic. I cannot practice one without the other. Absolutely can not. I believe Kenneth Rexroth was like that. His was a Catholicism of great intellectual depth. For years he studied and wrote about Thomas Aquinas.

Here's something I personally find to be true: Buddhism is a religion for ordinary life, and Christianity is a religion for crises. In my daily life Zen is the predominant practice until I am in crisis. The instant that crisis hits ... Philomene in no longer sitting crosslegged in front of a statue of a serene Buddha. She is on her knees before her enormous wooden cross (one that opens up and contains all the ingredients to perform the Last Rites).

Levi: What's your favorite poem you've ever written?

Philomene: "La Purisima" used to be my favorite poem because of how it came through me. Pure – directly from the source to the page. After writing it, I changed only one word.

"La Purisima" means "The Pure" – a Latin term used for Mary, the Mother of God. Although the poem is giving voice to a California Mission, it is also a self portrait of sorts:

La Purisima

I am not here
Bent, brittle
Weed among weeds
Not here
Palms fragrant with lavender
Hair meandering through
The pale grasses
I can no longer remember
I preferred all martyrdoms
To this dry, silent place
There were nights when I feared
My own blood. My eyes
Became wounds. They devoured
Me. And the flies. Ten thousand
Tangled devils. My palms scoured
Dry and thin as communion wafers.
There were nights when the hymns I sang
Became the bones of the Friar, the dust
Upon the graves of stillborn Indians
The winds of La Purisima
Through the pale grassed

A LITERARY GENERATION'S LEGACY

I can no longer remember

My current favorite poem, and one I now live with, is: "Pieta In Los Angeles, Part 2". It's a meditation before a replica of Michelangelo's Pieta.

For two years after my husband John Thomas's death, my greatest solace was to stand before a replica sculpture of the Pieta, which is down the hall from where John is entombed at Holy Cross Cemetery. I would look upon the Pieta until I became the Pieta.

Pieta in Los Angeles, Part 2

The marble corpus dangles
Precariously over the Mother's lap
Her right hand alone supports him
Fingers splayed, deep into his rib cage
Her knees apart
As one would balance an infant
Above him, her soft breasts
Seemingly turn marble into flesh

His hair thick with blood
Blood into stone
Lips parted in death
Hers pressed gently in speechless grief

The folds of her dress
Run through his fingers
It is almost as if he reaches for her
From his now mute anguish

Her back is straight, head slightly bent
A thin line across her forehead
In her face, a grieving so severe
It becomes serenity

Her left upturned palm
Opened to receive the world's sorrow
Is at once: a question and acceptance

I reach up
Place my tear-soaked tissue in that hand
In my mind I would climb into the lap
But no, not for me
Not that comfort yet
Must first become
That hand
That face
Become
Rock of sorrow
Eternity in granite
Time and agony
In stone

Later I say that I must become that hand, that face.

Levi: How did you meet John Thomas?

Philomene: We met the morning I was born. This is fact.

John fell in love with me after attending a poetry reading on
March 15 ("the ides of March"), 1983 at the "Come Back Inn" in
Venice. John had said, "You certainly have not lost your youthful
exuberance." And then "I don't agree with what you just said, but

237

I appreciate how you said it." And laughed. At the beginning of the laugh he was not in love. At the end of that laugh he was in love.

We first kissed in the parking spot besides the old Venice jail.

I realized I was in love with John a few weeks later on April 6, 1983, while walking down the Venice Boardwalk with a dozen pink roses in my arms. People stopped what we were doing or saying and stared – looking at me as if I were in love. I thought: "I must be in love."

We made love for the first time on Good Friday, 1983, at 3:00 pm. 19 years later John would die on Good Friday, 2002, at 3:00pm.

Levi: You and John were close friends with Charles Bukowski. Can you share something about him?

Philomene: Since a focus of your piece is religion, I'll share this, an excerpt from 8 hours of audio tapes of conversations recorded by John:

> *John Thomas: (Singing) "Jesus loves me this I know for the Bible tells me so."*
>
> *Charles Bukowski: I like spiritual songs when they're really well done.*
>
> *John: That's not spiritual.*

Bukowski: Yeah, I know.

*John: That's a little Sunday school hymn.
(Singing) "Carry your Bible with you."*

*Bukowski: I heard one on the radio driving on the
way to the racetrack. Something like Jesus on the
cross and it was beautiful. And they got his hands
nailed to the cross and how beautiful it was. And I
thought, "These words are good." These weren't
the exact words, but I translated it that way and I
said, "Jesus, this is good." How beautiful – how
they got those spikes in his hands and they're all
singing. God! How beautiful.*

A LITERARY GENERATION'S LEGACY

ABOUT LITERARY KICKS

Literary Kicks was founded in July 23, 1994 as an online tribute to the Beat Generation writers, primarily Jack Kerouac, Allen Ginsberg, Neal Cassady and William S. Burroughs. Originally launched without any long-term plan at all, the website quickly grew in size and popularity and was nominated for a Webby award in 1998.

In 2001, Litkicks transformed itself into a message-based community website with poetry boards and active discussion areas on diverse literary topics. In 2004 it transformed itself again into a literary blog. The site remains popular around the world, and continues to publish online articles and works in other formats (such as this book) relating to literature, society, philosophy and pop culture.

10114555R00142

Made in the USA
San Bernardino, CA
07 April 2014